Honey's

NATURAL
FEEDING HANDBOOK
for Dogs

Jonathan Self

The
Mammoth
Publishing Company

First published in 2012
The Mammoth Publishing Company
An imprint of Wentworth Publishing Limited
17 Fleet Street, London EC4 Y1AA
Telephone 020 7353 7300
Web: www.mammothpublishing.com
ISBN: 978-0-9570753-0-6

For Tom Farrington and Vicky Marshall

HONEY'S NATURAL FEEDING HANDBOOK FOR DOGS

Contents

1.

HOW TO TRANSFORM YOUR DOG'S HEALTH WITH A SIMPLE CHANGE OF DIET

ONE

The connection between good health and diet is well established in humans. We know that if we eat fresh fruit, fresh vegetables, not too much dairy and moderate quantities of animal protein we will live longer, healthier lives. We also know that if we eat processed food or food containing chemical additives, too much fat and too much sugar we will live shorter, considerably less healthy lives.

In fact, it is well proven that everything from allergies to heart conditions and from skin complaints to cancer is caused by a poor diet. What holds good for humans and human food holds good for dogs and dog food. Dogs that eat a natural diet live longer, healthier lives. The problem is that we have lost touch with what the natural, correct diet for a dog actually is. Instead, we feed them the canine equivalent of junk food.

As a result we are seeing more and more illness in our dogs and they are leading shorter and shorter lives. The development of all sorts of genetic conditions may also be attributable to generations of dogs eating a harmful diet.

Happily, the situation can be quickly and effortlessly corrected. We know what a biologically appropriate diet for dogs is and it couldn't be easier to replicate a 'wild' diet using 'tame' ingredients. Furthermore, as those who have switched their dogs to a natural diet will testify, the results can be amazing.

Benefits include a glossy coat, healthy skin, lean muscle tone, robust immune system, sweet-smelling breath, healthy teeth and gums, increased energy, better digestion and a strong heart.

Dogs eating a raw food diet can be expected to live longer and to suffer less illness and disease.

Indeed, if your dog has any health issues now (even minor problems such as allergies, dry skin, bad breath and what the

Americans refer to, euphemistically, as 'gas') it is quite likely that a switch to a raw food diet will clear them up.

This handbook explains why your dog will be better off on a natural diet and provides simple instructions on how to prepare his or her food yourself.

I have written it because although there are some excellent books on raw feeding I couldn't find a short, plain-English, practical guide to the subject.

It is based on my own experience as the founder of an artisan dog food business (Honey's Real Dog Food), which is responsible for raw feeding over 4,000 dogs a month.

If you have any questions or need additional help, please do remember that my colleagues and I are always happy to assist in any way we can. I must stress you don't ever have to become a customer to take advantage of our knowledge and advice. You'll find our contact details on the back cover of the book.

2.
A BLUFFER'S GUIDE TO
NATURAL FEEDING

TWO

Pressed for time but keen to understand the basics of natural feeding? Here is a summary of all the main points made in this book. Everything, in fact, that you need to know to bluff your way with the best.

Dogs should be fed a biologically appropriate diet

Every creature on earth must consume the diet it is biologically most appropriate to eat; otherwise, it will get ill and may (if the diet is really inappropriate) die. For the first 4 million years of dogs' existence on earth they certainly didn't eat canned food or kibble. Four million years? Yes, that's how long grey wolves have been around, and dogs and wolves are classified as the same species. When wolves were domesticated (around 8,000-20,000 years ago), we humans changed their outer appearance through breeding, but not their internal organs or digestive systems.

In the wild, dogs eat prey and not much else

Dogs are carnivores (they do need a bit of herbage and if push comes to shove can survive on it) as even a cursory glance at their anatomy reveals. Like other predatory mammals they have powerful muscles, fused wrist bones and a cardiovascular system that supports both sprinting and endurance. And there's a reason why you don't want to get bitten by a dog: their mouths are positive Swiss Army knives, with five kinds of exceedingly sharp teeth. Leave them to their own devices and they will eat small birds and beasts (rabbits, mice, squirrels &c.) and a share of larger prey (sheep, deer, boar &c.). What's more, they eat the whole animal, including its bones.

Canine digestion is nothing like human digestion

Dogs have no digestive enzymes in their saliva (unlike humans) and very large, expandable stomachs (they can eat 5% of their body weight at a single sitting, which would be like someone who weighs 10 stone eating seven pounds of food in one go) not to mention indescribably strong stomach acids (strong enough to burn your fingers). Their digestive system is designed so that they can tear off chunks of raw meat, crunch up raw bones and swallow the lot whole. The lack of digestive enzymes in their saliva and their inability to move their jaws from side to side (necessary to grinding food) is why they gulp everything down. The entire digestive process takes place in their stomach.

Give a dog a bone

In the wild up to a third of a dog's nutrition (including calcium, magnesium, complex fats and vitamins) may come from bones. Bones keep their teeth and gums clean (it has been proven that dogs with healthy teeth live longer) and exercise their upper bodies and jaw. Providing the bones are raw (cooked bones can splinter), they are 100% safe for dogs to eat.

Dogs are extremely indifferent cooks

When food is cooked, its chemical structure is altered and most of the enzymes, amino acids and so forth are destroyed. From a dog's perspective, about 70% of its nutritional value is thus lost. Dogs need their food served raw in order to digest it properly. There is a reason why dogs are extremely indifferent cooks.

Dog poo

Natural feeders talk a lot about poo. Dogs fed a natural diet produce very little of it, what there is being firm and chalky.

Dogs don't eat regular, balanced meals

Regular, balanced meals are fine for humans, but not for dogs. In the wild a healthy dog may not eat for up to a week at a time. When they come across an ingredient that their bodies tell them they need in order to stay healthy (for instance a particular grass containing useful trace minerals) they simply eat it. Dogs are designed to get the nutrition they require over time. This is called the 'balance over time' approach.

What is wrong with processed dog food?

It doesn't matter which brand of dog food you use or how much it costs, it is never going to be as good for your dog as raw, fresh meat, bone and vegetable. The key problems are:

- It is cooked. Cooking destroys the vast majority of the nutritional value of the food from a dog's perspective and makes it exceedingly difficult to digest.
- It can contain inappropriate and damaging chemicals (binders, colouring, preservatives and other additives). These may be absorbed through the bowel wall and transported to other organs, with a range of harmful effects.
- The quality of the ingredients is usually poor. Even expensive dog food often has very, very low-quality ingredients.
- Most dog foods contain a high percentage of grain (including rice), which is unsuitable for the canine digestive system and causes allergies.
- It generally fails to clean the dog's teeth and gums, allowing plaque to build up. This gives rise to periodontal disease and worse.

Dogs can't digest grain

Dogs must not be fed grain, because they can't digest it properly. One of the main reasons why dogs fed on processed food produce so much – ahem – waste matter is because of the grain. Grain is also one of the main causes of skin allergies, diabetes and flatulence.

The switch

Natural feeders sometimes refer to the time they moved their dog onto raw food as 'the switch'. The longer ago you made the switch, the more you will be respected in raw feeding circles. The switch itself can usually be made instantly. A very small percentage of dogs have to be weaned onto raw food but the vast majority take to it immediately. The only dogs that shouldn't eat a 100% raw diet are those with a compromised immune system or those that have just undergone bowel surgery. More about this later.

The BARF movement

If you are going to bluff your way in natural feeding, you will hear a great deal about the BARF diet, which is the same thing. BARF stands for Biologically Appropriate Raw Food, a rather revolting acronym thought up by a brilliant Australian vet called Ian Billinghurst. The other big natural feeding hero is Tom Lonsdale (also a vet), who heads up the Raw Meaty Bones lobby.

It couldn't be easier to feed raw

As a bluffer you will want a simple recipe. Try 80% raw, lean-ish meat and 20% grated or puréed raw vegetables (but not potato). The meat can be anything – chicken, lamb, beef, rabbit, pork, venison, squirrel, whatever – and you can mince it or serve it in chunks. Include a bit of offal. From time to time add in the odd egg, spoon of oil (cod liver, for instance), tin of pilchards, spoon of natural yoghurt &c. Make sure your dog gets plenty of raw bones – chicken wings will do if that's easier for you.

3.
THE MYSTERIES OF CANINE DIGESTION REVEALED

A WOLF IN ALL BUT NAME

If you look up dogs in any encyclopaedia you will see that their Latin classification is *Canis lupus familiaris* and that they are a domesticated form of the grey wolf, aka *Canis lupus lupus*.

In other words, they are the same species.

The grey wolf has been in existence for over four million years but domesticated wolves (dogs) have only been around for some 8,000–20,000 years.

Whether humans captured wolves and domesticated them or wolves domesticated themselves is not clear. Possibly a bit of both.

What is certain is that from early on we selectively bred dogs with a view to developing certain physical and behavioural traits. Thus, over time, we created hunting dogs, retrieving dogs, guard dogs, companion dogs and so forth.

We may have managed to alter the way dogs look and, to a certain extent, think, but physiologically they haven't changed.

There is absolutely no difference (apart from size) between the internal organs and digestive process of a Chihuahua and a grey wolf.

This is why they should eat the same diet.

THREE

The bond between humans and dogs is so close that it is easy to forget that, being different species, we have markedly different digestive systems. Dogs actually have the same digestive system as the grey wolf and, therefore, need to eat the same diet.

The word 'need' is worth stressing. Every living creature on earth must eat a biologically appropriate diet. Some species have a greater tolerance than others, but no species thrives on an incorrect diet and many become ill and die. It is possible for a species to partially adapt to a new diet. Palaeontologists believe that this change takes at least 100,000 years.

Meat glorious meat

Dogs are carnivores. True, they can and do eat vegetable matter, but anatomically they are designed to catch, kill and eat prey.

As with other predatory mammals, they have powerful muscles relative to their size, fused wrist bones and a cardiovascular system that supports both sprinting and endurance.

And a quick look inside their mouth is all it takes to understand why they are really much, much closer to being carnivores than omnivores.

Your dog's mouth is a bit like a Swiss Army knife

No matter how sweet and innocent a dog may look, the inside of his or her mouth tells a different story.

Dogs have five types of teeth, each designed to perform different and precise functions: fang teeth to catch and kill prey and to tear off meat; front teeth to scrape meat off bones; small incisors to grab and hold; large incisors that work like scissors to cut sinews and muscles; and molars to crush bones. None of these teeth, however, is capable of grinding food.

Indeed, if you gently try to move a dog's jaw from side to side (necessary for grinding and chewing) you'll find that it is impossible.

A dog's jaw can only move up and down.

All the action takes place in the stomach

A dog's digestive process starts in its stomach. This differs dramatically from humans. We use our teeth to grind our food and moisten it with saliva containing digestive enzymes so that the digestive process is well in hand by the time we swallow.

Dogs, on the other hand, don't have any digestive enzymes in their saliva and even if they did it would be useless because they can't grind their food, owing to having jaws that only open and close.

Instead, they gulp their food with a view to getting it to where the action takes place (the stomach) as quickly as possible.

What happens when the food arrives?

The stomach starts to produce digestive enzymes and other chemicals to break it down into small molecules that can be absorbed and used by the body. Some of these enzymes are produced by the pancreas, but many are produced by other small glands in the stomach wall itself.

To help the digestive process dogs have extremely strong and corrosive stomach acids. Acidity is measured using something called pH. Neutral is pH 7, but when a dog is digesting food its stomach operates between pH 1 and pH 2. Put in plain English: if you touched the natural acids in a dog's stomach, you would burn your fingers.

Another important point in relation to this is that most enzymes are extremely sensitive to pH and won't function in the wrong environment. If a dog eats inappropriate food then its digestive system can't function properly.

Dogs have evolved to eat a lot, quite quickly

Dogs can consume up to 5% of their body weight in an extremely short period. To put this into perspective, it would be like a 10-stone human eating, say, seven pounds of food in a single sitting.

A dog's stomach looks rather like an accordion with lots of folds. It expands when full and its muscles massage the food to ensure that the digestive juices work properly. Once all the digestible pieces of food have been dissolved, the muscles squeeze the now liquid mass into the intestine for the final stage of the process and for the absorption of the nutrients. A dog's stomach is designed to finish digesting one meal before being filled again. This process generally takes longer than for humans, although it very much depends on what the dog has eaten.

Why dogs should eat a natural diet

Every species should eat what it is biologically designed to eat, in other words what it would eat in the wild or as close to what it would eat as is feasible.

Dogs are, essentially, wolves and, as such, are designed to catch, kill and eat prey. They have a markedly different digestive system from humans and shouldn't eat the same diet as us, any more than we should eat the same diet as a cow.

4.
WHAT DOGS EAT
(AND DON'T EAT)
IN THE WILD

THE GRAIN PROBLEM

Why shouldn't dogs be fed grain? The answer lies in its effect on the pH balance in their stomachs. Normally (see the previous chapter) this is quite low (between pH 1 and pH 2) because only with a low pH can dogs digest raw meat and bones. Grain has the effect of elevating the pH level and weakening the stomach acids. Weak stomach acids mean that proper digestion becomes impossible.

This is why dogs fed a lot of grain (and there is a lot of grain in most processed dog food) produce high levels of waste matter. It goes in one end and comes out the other.

If grain is processed in some way (rolled, soaked, heated &c.) dogs can digest a small amount, which is what dog food manufacturers rely upon.

Even so, there is another issue. We humans can eat carbohydrates (such as porridge or pasta), convert them to sugars and store the energy in our bodies to use later on. Dogs have no capacity to do this. Grain (rice, wheat, corn &c.) is much cheaper than meat and easier to process, which is why so much of it is used in manufactured dog food.

FOUR

As already discussed, every species should eat a biologically appropriate diet, in other words what they would eat in the wild or as close to what they would eat in the wild as is feasible. In the case of dogs there is quite a lot of variety in their natural diet.

What dogs eat in the wild

Dogs are carnivores and the primary component of their diet is prey. This could be small animals – mice, voles, rabbits, birds, insects and so forth – or it could be larger prey caught with the help of a pack. Either way, they eat everything – the internal organs, the meat, the bones... the lot.

Dogs aren't obligate carnivores like cats (see Chapter 15). They can and do eat vegetable matter.

Wild dogs will search for rotten fruit and will eat the semi-digested contents of their prey's stomach. Some will dig up vegetables and eat grasses and herbs.

Dogs are also scavengers. They eat the leftovers from every animal that is killed or dies. As Ian Billinghurst, a leading proponent of natural feeding, has pointed out, dogs receive 'valuable nutrients from materials that we humans find totally repugnant. Things like vomit, faeces and decaying flesh.'

With regard to the faeces, incidentally, these contain the dead and living bodies of millions upon billions of bacteria. They are an excellent source of protein, essential fatty acids, fat-soluble vitamins, minerals, antioxidants, enzymes and fibre.

Not wanting to dwell on an unpleasant subject, but if you have a dog that is on a processed food diet he or she may be eating faeces in order to try to stay healthy (although if a dog is eating canine or feline faeces it will probably be because they contain the undigested flavourings used to make them palatable).

What dogs don't eat in the wild

Almost as important as what dogs eat in the wild is what they don't eat.

For starters (as it were), they don't necessarily eat every day. Depending on where they live, the season, the size of the pack, the available prey and other factors, they may eat as infrequently as every second or third day or even longer without suffering any ill effect. A healthy dog can go a week without food.

Second, and perhaps more important, they don't eat 'complete' meals. Dogs meet their nutritional requirements over time. They will eat what they need or seek it out if their body is telling them they need it.

This is referred to as the 'balance over time' concept. It is crucial to the way dogs should be fed because there is evidence that dogs fed all the ingredients they need in proportion at every meal suffer increased health problems.

Finally, dogs don't eat grain. They can't digest it properly and, even if they could, they can't convert it into sugar and store it for later use.

REDUCE YOUR VET BILLS BY
UP TO 85%!

Mogens Eliasen, in his book *Raw Food for Dogs*, quotes a major Australian study on natural feeding. He points out that 'dogs fed on a natural diet develop a strong immune system that will cause your vet bills to go down, maybe even dramatically'. He goes on to remark that the kennels which switched from feeding kibble to raw food 'experienced a significant reduction in their vet bills' with the average saving being 85%! In other words, where they were spending £100 before, they now only spend £15. As explained elsewhere in this handbook, dogs on a natural diet have also been shown to live on average a third longer.

5.

GIVE A DOG A BONE

FIVE

'The first time a vet suggested giving our dog a bone to chew on I was slightly shocked,' admits Vicky Marshall, the cofounder of Honey's Real Dog Food. 'This, I thought to myself, borders on malpractice. The poor dog will choke or, worse, he will swallow a bit of bone and then… well, I wasn't quite sure what might happen but I felt certain nothing good could come of it.'

Vicky's initial reaction was by no means uncommon. She had bought into the myth, promoted by the pet food industry, that the only food suitable for dogs was manufactured food, that is to say canned food, dried food, pouched food and a range of treats that included, ironically, fake bones.

Processed dog food is bad for dogs on all sorts of grounds: it is cooked, usually contains lots of grains, uses poor-quality meat and is packed full of preservatives and other harmful chemicals. Its worst failing, however, is that no matter how hard the manufacturers try to replicate the goodness of a natural diet it can't match the benefits offered by a raw, meaty bone.

In the wild, dogs eat their prey, bones and all

Nature knows best. It is one of those trite things that people say, but, when one stops to think about it, the phrase contains a great truth. In the wild, providing they have a choice, all animals eat what is best for them. For dogs this means small prey or, if hunting in a pack, a share of larger prey. They are thrifty, too. Nothing is wasted and that includes the bones. Initially these are ripped, torn, chewed and sucked to remove all the meat and marrow. Then they are gnawed, crunched and (if small enough) eaten whole.

There has been some fantastically interesting (if gory) research in Australia proving this, in which scientists studied the insides of hundreds of wild dogs (don't even ask). One study was by a chap called S. J. O. Whitehouse (*Australian Wildlife Research* magazine, 1977, 4(2): 145–50); another, by a chap called A. E. Newsome (*Australian Wildlife Research* magazine, 1983, 10(3): 477–86). Hundreds of dogs were examined across a wide geographical area. The results were conclusive not only on the bone issue, by the way, but also on other dietary preferences. No wild dog, for example, ever eats grain.

(Note there is more research available on the same topic, including detailed studies by Neville Buck, who studied a wide range of dogs and wolves at Howletts and Port Lympne Wild Animal Parks in the UK.)

Bones are packed full of vital nutrients

It is easy to understand why the dog wants the meat and marrow, but what makes the bone itself so desirable? The answer is that bones contain a huge number of nutrients that are vital to your dog's health. These include:

- minerals, including calcium, magnesium and phosphorous
- protein-containing essential amino acids, including lysine
- essential fatty acids
- fat-soluble vitamins (A, D and E)
- blood-forming nutrients (these are in the marrow), including copper and iron.

Bones keep your dog's teeth and gums healthy

Meaty bones are nature's toothbrushes. They keep your dog's teeth clean and gums healthy. Plaque can't build up and decay is prevented. As a result your dog shouldn't develop any of the nasty oral diseases to which many of those on processed food are prone. It will also mean he or she has sweeter breath.

You may be interested to know that a growing number of vets believe that there is a close connection between oral health and general health. One veterinary dentist who has studied this is Dr Gary Beard, who is based at Auburn University in Alabama. In 1991, he wrote a paper pointing out that heart failure, hepatic compromise, renal failure and other serious diseases in dogs could be a direct result of poor oral hygiene. The same year another US vet, Dr Richard Hamlin, of Ohio State University, proposed that diseases of the heart, liver and lungs could be caused this way.

Bones provide great exercise, and help with mental health

Two further benefits of giving your dog bones should be mentioned:

- They provide your dog with exercise, strengthening their jaws and upper body.
- They keep your dog occupied. Dogs that have a bone to chew are happier and calmer.

A word about marrow bones

Dogs love marrow bones – the marrow being the creamy centre in the middle of the bone. The upside of marrow is that it is high in nutritional value, the downside is that it is high in fat. If you are feeding a dog that is trying to lose weight then either scoop the marrow out or choose another type of bone.

BONE FEEDING TIPS

- Dogs love bones from pretty much any animal or bird you care to mention.
- A good bone to start with is a beef marrowbone. Ask the butcher to cut it to the right size for your dog: too large to be swallowed in a single gulp, small enough to handle.
- Chicken wings and carcasses (yes, carcasses!) are excellent, too.
- Only feed raw bones. When a bone is cooked, it hardens and may splinter.
- Choose bones from young animals. Most bones you obtain from a butcher are bound to be from a younger animal, but it is worth checking. Older animals (and birds) may have harder bones, again more likely to splinter.
- The first time you give your dog a raw bone, stay around to watch. Inexperienced dogs can become overexcited and there is a slim possibility of choking. For this reason a large, meaty knucklebone is perfect. Lamb bones and especially ribs, although excellent, can get caught in the mouth and should only be fed to more experienced dogs. Also, hooves are not a good idea as they can splinter.

6.
THE UNPALATABLE TRUTH ABOUT PROCESSED DOG FOOD

HOW MODERN DOG FOOD CAME TO BE INVENTED

A good way to understand the dog food industry is to study its history.

Modern dog food was invented by James Spratt, an American living in England, who launched the first complete dog food – a biscuit made of wheat meal, vegetables and blood – in 1860. Almost immediately mill owners saw its potential as a way of selling their by-products (basically floor sweepings) and low-cost meat meal at a much higher price than they would otherwise achieve.

From day one, dog food producers made extravagant claims for their products and paid vets for endorsements. Interestingly, the basic recipe for dried dog food, manufacturers' claims and the marketing methods have barely changed at all in over 150 years.

Ken-L-Ration, the first canned dog food, was launched after the First World War, when oversupply led to horsemeat becoming almost worthless. Demand grew and by the end of the 1960s all but a tiny percentage of dogs living in developed nations came to be fed on manufactured dog food. Perhaps this isn't surprising when one thinks how consumers moved from old-fashioned cooking to modern convenience foods.

SIX

If the television commercials, advertisements and labelling are to be believed, processed food is the only safe thing to feed a dog. It contains nothing but natural goodness, has been scientifically formulated and is endorsed by experts, including vets. What's more, if your dog is suffering from any particular ailment, there is almost certainly a food designed to put it right. Pet food manufacturers would have it that they are your dog's best friend. After reading this chapter you may begin to feel otherwise. Indeed, you may conclude that you have been misled and deceived.

The law doesn't protect dogs

There is a considerable volume of British and European legislation controlling the manufacture of dog food but it barely considers the health of the animals eating it. Its real purpose is to protect the human food chain. This quote (the italics are mine), taken from the guidance given to pet food manufacturers, demonstrates how little the government cares:

> For pets, the main part of the risk assessment when setting the maximum permitted levels for *undesirable substances* will generally be the extent to which the animal can tolerate them.

In other words, it is legal to use *undesirable substances* in dog food providing they don't kill the animal immediately.

Another disturbing quote from the same guide refers to ingredients:

> The material of animal origin used by the pet food industry comprises those parts of animals which are either deemed surplus to human consumption or are not normally consumed by people in the UK, and derived from animals inspected and passed as fit for human consumption *prior to slaughter*. Animal material of this nature, which is not intended for human consumption, is classified as *animal by-products* under the EC Regulation.

This innocuous statement allows manufacturers to make their food from so-called *by-products*, that is to say hooves, tails, testicles, ears and other bits of animal. It also authorises them to use ingredients that are not suitable for human consumption. How so? If the *by-products* or meat come from an animal that was fit for human consumption *prior to slaughter*, that's fine. The meat could be a year old and completely rotten for all the legislators care.

The notes about labelling are also revealing:

> The labelling requirements for pet food are less onerous than those for feed for farmed livestock [for humans]. For livestock, the ingredients must be declared individually in descending order by weight, but pet food manufacturers have the option to declare them by category – e.g., 'meat and animal derivatives', 'oils and fats', 'cereals', 'vegetable protein extracts'.

The significance of this is huge, as it allows manufacturers to hide the actual ingredients being used in their dog food.

A licence to print money

It isn't just that the legislation doesn't consider canine health; it is entirely skewed in the manufacturers' favour. As you can see from the quotes above, they can put in almost any ingredient they want (providing it doesn't actually poison the dog) and can be misleading in what they tell consumers. How did this happen? Since the industry came into being, manufacturers have managed to persuade both the public and legislators that they are experts and can be trusted. They have used clever marketing techniques and veterinary endorsements to great effect and have been much aided by consumer demand for convenience.

It also helps that for many years the industry has been dominated by five multinational corporations, which between them control around 80% of the worldwide market. They are Nestlé's (Purina, Bakers &c.), Del Monte (the Heinz range of pet foods), MasterFoods/Mars (Royal Canin, Pedigree &c.), Procter & Gamble (Iams, Eukanuba &c.) and Colgate-Palmolive (Hill's Science Diet, Nature's Best &c.).

These companies lobby hard to ensure that their business interests aren't disturbed by unhelpful legislation. Their biggest single market is the USA, where pet food accounts for $15 billion a year. But the UK market is still sizeable with over £1 billion a year spent on dog food alone.

It isn't just the overall size of the market that makes it so attractive to manufacturers. Processed dog food is incredibly profitable. As one commentator pointed out:

> What most consumers don't realise is that the pet food industry is an extension of the human food and agriculture industries. Pet food provides a convenient way for slaughterhouse offal, grains considered unfit for human consumption and similar waste products to be turned into profit.

Why processed food is so bad for dogs

Low-quality ingredients

Processed dog food is generally made using extremely low-quality ingredients. As explained elsewhere in this chapter, that means animal by-products and derivatives and low-quality grain.

It has been cooked

Processed food has been cooked. Cooking alters the food's chemical structure, destroys much of its nutritional value and makes it extremely difficult for a dog to digest (see Chapter 3 on canine digestion for more information). A processed food diet, because it is cooked, forces the pancreas to work harder and to draw other enzymes from the bloodstream. This can leave a dog physically vulnerable because the enzymes in the blood are supposed to be protecting the body, not aiding digestion. A number of medical studies show that the pancreas enlarges on a diet of processed food. An enlarged organ means excessive function. Excessive function can lead to degeneration. It is a similar story when it comes to amino acids. Cooking at high temperatures alters the arrangement of these acids, making half of them unusable by the canine body.

Manufacturers try to persuade consumers that the canine digestive system has altered and can now accommodate cooked and processed food. Palaeontologists estimate that a period of at least 100,000 years is required before evolutionary changes occur within a whole species. The most accepted theories estimate that dogs began their association with humans between 8,000 and 20,000 years ago. They haven't, therefore, had time to adapt to eating cooked food let alone processed food, which has only been around since 1860!

In the case of kibble it is also too concentrated and too dry (less than 10% moisture compared to 70% moisture in a natural diet).

It contains grain

Grain is used a great deal in processed food as it is inexpensive and gives it bulk. Some food will contain up to 65% grain, although this may not be apparent from the labelling. In the wild less than 1% of a dog's diet will be grain. There is a reason why one rarely sees a dog stalking a wheat or rice field. Complex carbohydrates (grains) that dogs eat just end up in an accumulation of lactic acids. Whereas humans can convert complex carbohydrates into sugars and store them for use later (this is what happens when one eats, say, porridge), dogs can't do either. Most grain in processed dog food ends up going in one end and coming out the other.

It contains fibre

Processed food contains a high percentage of fibre, described as 'crude fibre' because it is of such low quality. In most cases the fibre takes the form of peanut hulls, almond shells, empty grain hulls, beet pulp and so forth. None of these things offers any nutritional value to dogs.

It contains preservatives

Chemical preservatives are added to keep the food from going off. Where there are no added preservatives, it is either because the food has been heated to such a high temperature that no preservatives are necessary or because the original ingredients already contained sufficient preservatives.

It contains artificial colouring

Dried and canned food is usually grey. For this reason food colouring is added to give it a more natural appearance. Many trainers believe that the artificial colouring is one of the causes of behavioural issues in dogs.

WHAT ARE ANIMAL BY-PRODUCTS AND DERIVATIVES?

The term 'animal by-products' refers to heads, hooves, feet, viscera and other animal parts you may prefer not to think about. The term 'animal derivatives' refers to heart, lung, muscle meat, testicles and so forth.

Manufacturers can claim that food is 'organic' and even 'fit for human consumption' but that doesn't mean that the ingredients are of high quality. A lung from an organic cow falls into both these categories but you wouldn't necessarily want to eat it. If you would like to know more about this topic visit: www.pet-food-choice.co.uk.

It contains binders

In the manufacturing process many of the ingredients in dog food are rendered, that is to say they are heated until they turn into a liquid. In order to make it look like kibble or 'chunks of meat' chemical binders are added.

It contains unhealthy fats

Many commercial dog foods have fat sprayed on them as a way of making them palatable. Fat may also be added to improve nutritional value. The quality of this fat is usually poor. Fat can be recycled from deep fryers in restaurants and tallow that rises from rendering plants. It may be rancid.

Up to 9 out of 10 canine health issues may be caused by diet

A growing number of vets and nutritionists believe that many if not most of the medical conditions that dogs are being treated for nowadays are a direct result of their diet. Tom Farrington, Honey's Chief Veterinary Surgeon, considers as many as 9 out of 10 canine health issues – everything from relatively minor problems such as bad breath, flatulence, itchiness, allergies and dry skin through to major problems such as cancer, liver disease, heart disease and kidney disease – may be directly related to processed food. As Ian Billinghurst, author of *Give Your Dog a Bone*, says:

> Our dogs' disease problems are increasing on a par with their increasing consumption of processed and cooked foods … dog food manufacturers take useless waste from the human food industry and sell it as dog food. Why do they bother? Advertising implies that they are there to promote the health of dogs. Their primary concern is in fact profit. The laws which govern dog food production do not require it to promote health, reproduction, growth or longevity.

If one cares about dogs it is very easy to get worked up about the processed dog food industry. It is a scandal waiting to happen. The only difference between this situation and what occurred with tobacco, asbestos, powdered milk formula, fast food and all the other consumer campaigns that have led to major changes is that the victims of the processed dog food industry can't speak for themselves.

How long will consumers (and their dogs) put up with the lies?

There's an Australian study (quoted by Mogens Eliasen) in which it was demonstrated that a dog's life expectancy increased by 30% when fed a raw, natural diet. Dogs that normally were expected to live until age 12 maintained a healthy life until they were 16 years old. This rather implies that dogs fed a processed food diet are leading shorter lives. Which, in turn, begs the question: how long can manufacturers of harmful processed food get away with their lies?

WATCH OUT FOR 'PALATABILITY ENHANCERS'

The leading raw food expert, Mogens Eliasen, warns against another rarely discussed ingredient in processed food: palatability enhancers:

> Manufacturing of these chemicals is a whole industry on its own, supporting the pet food manufacturers with drugs that both taste good and make the animal addicted to the food, once it gets a taste of it. It is literally no different than giving a teenager cocaine or heroin in order to create a customer for more drugs.

7.

VETS AND RAW FEEDING

FINDING A GOOD VET

Our Chief Veterinary Surgeon is a member of the British Association of Homeopathic Veterinary Surgeons (BAHVS). Most members are not only in favour of raw feeding but also actively promote it. If you were looking for a really good vet we would certainly recommend you start here: www.bahvs.com.

Two other professional bodies whose members are more inclined to support raw feeding are the British Association of Veterinary Herbalists (www.herbalvets.org.uk) and the British Association of Veterinary Acupuncturists (www.abva.co.uk).

If you are looking for a forward-thinking, holistic vet, please do contact Honey's. We keep a list in the office.

SEVEN

Given the irrefutable fact that the biologically appropriate diet for dogs consists of raw meat, bones and vegetables, you may be surprised to hear that a high percentage of vets are either ambivalent towards or openly against the diet.

Why, when dogs have been eating raw food for millions of years, should highly educated and, one would hope, caring professionals take such a stance?

The reasons are various and complex.

It isn't easy being a vet

It takes vets seven years to qualify, after which they will probably spend a year or two gaining experience in someone else's practice before starting up on their own.

When they do set up, they will have to invest heavily in building their surgery with no government support (unlike dentists and doctors).

Isolation, stress and high expectations from clients mean that vets suffer from above-average levels of depression and an above-average suicide rate. This probably isn't helped by the fact that part of their work requires them to euthanise animals on a regular basis.

They don't get rich, either. GPs earn, on average, over £100,000 a year. Vets earn, on average, closer to £30,000. It isn't easy being a vet.

The exploiters!

There are two, highly profitable, sectors that exploit vets.

The first is the pharmaceutical industry. The behaviour of pharmaceutical manufacturers need not concern us here, except it is worth remembering that it is not in their commercial interest for dogs and cats to be healthy.

The second is the pet food industry. Ever since pet food was invented (by one James Spratt in 1860), manufacturers have been getting vets to endorse and sell their products.

Pet food sales keep some vets afloat

For some time now, pet food manufacturers have been providing vets with financial support:

- They pay commission to vets for selling food via their surgeries.
- They pay vets to carry out 'research', attend conferences, write papers and so forth. They support several of the professional bodies.

With part of their income coming from pet food companies, it isn't surprising that many vets are inclined to believe what those manufacturers tell them about the suitability of their food.

The colleges are no less to blame

Vets can be forgiven for their lack of knowledge about raw feeding for another reason: they are taught very little about canine digestion in the course of their studies. Colleges rarely devote more than a day to the topic and the lectures are often sponsored by pet food manufacturers. You can guess how impartial such lectures are likely to be.

The dark side

Vets have a tough job and they do it for love, not for money. Still, there are a few vets (a minuscule percentage) who must know full well that if dogs didn't suffer as much as they do from diet-related health issues they would lose a vast percentage of their business. It could be argued that manufactured pet food is causing most of the health problems that vets and pharmaceutical companies are trying to cure and that the only losers are their canine patients.

The solution

If vets received larger grants when they studied so that they didn't leave full-time education with huge debts. If their education included more about canine digestion. If clients were willing to pay a little more for veterinary services. Well, it would put an end to an awful lot of suffering.

A WORD OF WARNING ABOUT KIBBLE...

Kibble can cause special health issues. Because it is so dry (5% to 10% moisture compared to 70% moisture in a natural diet) and so concentrated, it fails to stimulate the dog's gastrointestinal system. Because of this, it can be dangerous to feed the dog until it feels full. Instead, one must keep the dog constantly hungry.

8.
THE STORY OF BARF

EIGHT

The acronym used to describe the practice of raw feeding dogs is somewhat unfortunate: BARF. The word is defined in the *Oxford Dictionary* as 'slang vb (tr), to vomit', but in the canine world it stands for Biologically Appropriate Raw Food. The BARF diet is designed to replicate what dogs would eat in the wild, that is to say raw meat, raw bones and raw vegetables, herbs and fruits.

So, where does the BARF concept come from?

It really began in the 1930s when a veterinary student, Juliette de Bairacli Levy, questioned the conventional approach to veterinary medicine and decided to explore traditional remedies and, in particular, herbalism. An intrepid explorer, she travelled extensively throughout Eastern Europe, the Middle East and Africa, living for long periods with gypsies and peasant farmers and learning about the natural remedies they used to cure man and beast. The result was a series of groundbreaking books on animal care and livestock management.

One of de Bairacli Levy's earliest conclusions was that dogs were healthier if they ate a natural diet of raw food and fasted regularly. Her books were highly influential and helped to stem the growth of manufactured pet food. However, from the 1950s onwards shopping and eating habits in the West changed massively. The amount of time spent in the kitchen fell dramatically and there was a move to convenience and processed food. What went for humans went for the family pets, too. By the 1980s all but a tiny percentage of dogs were being fed dried, canned or pouched food.

The switch to convenience food was not universal and even while it was happening there were dissenting voices. In the field of veterinary science one of those dissenting voices was an Australian vet called Ian Billinghurst, who, in 1993, published a book called *Give Your Dog a Bone* in which he espoused the same principles established by de Bairacli Levy some 60 years earlier.

Billinghurst was one of the first vets to make the connection between canine health and diet. It may seem obvious now but at the time it went in the face of what was generally held to be true, namely that pet food manufacturers knew what was best. Billinghurst says in his first book that as he saw patient after patient coming in with the same, persistent health issues, all of which seemed almost impossible to treat, he suddenly realised that he should be focusing on prevention rather than cure. This, in turn, led him to consider possible causes and the role played by diet.

Who actually came up with the BARF acronym is not entirely clear but Billinghurst is generally credited and all his subsequent books (of which there are several) use the B word in their title.

At almost the same time as BARF started to take off another similar movement began to gain popularity. Its followers believe that the food we give our dogs shouldn't just be raw… it should be made up almost entirely of raw meaty bones. The Raw Meaty Bones lobby was spearheaded by a British vet living in Australia called Tom Lonsdale. He wrote a book called *Raw Meaty Bones: Promote Health*. This, in some respects, is a rather more useful book than Billinghurst's because Lonsdale goes to great lengths to quote the scientific evidence behind raw feeding. There have been a number of studies and, although logic says that raw feeding makes sense, it is reassuring to see that it is based on hard fact.

9.
A SIMPLE BUT EFFECTIVE FEEDING PLAN FOR ADULT DOGS

NINE

Switching a dog to a natural diet couldn't be simpler and if you are concerned that raw feeding will be complicated, time-consuming, risky or expensive please put such thoughts right out of your mind:

- All you need to know to be a successful raw feeder is what ingredients are suitable for your dog and in roughly what proportions.
- With a little bit of planning it won't take you any more time than opening a can.
- Dogs are biologically designed to eat raw food and it is 100% safe for them to do so (remember: their stomach acids are so strong that they would burn your fingers).
- Your dog doesn't need prime steak! He or she will thrive on all sorts of inexpensive ingredients, as explained below.

Unless your dog has certain health issues (see below), there's no reason not to make a straight switch. Having said this, there are a few dogs (maybe one in a hundred) who don't take to natural feeding immediately, in which case you'll want to read the next chapter.

Incidentally, if you can withstand the looks of reproach it is no bad idea to fast your dog for a day before the switch. This will help your dog to rid its body of toxins built up while on a diet of processed food.

A simple three-step plan

Our straightforward feeding plan for adult dogs is a summary of decades of experience and it rests on three basic ingredients:

1. raw meat
2. raw bone
3. raw vegetable

The plan itself can be distilled into three simple steps:

1. Take any meat (chicken, beef, lamb, pork, whatever) minced or diced.
2. Grate vegetables into it (anything but potato) so that it is roughly ⅔ meat and ⅓ vegetable (you can put the vegetable through the food processor if you have one).
3. Get some meaty bones from the butcher and give your dog one every day or two (see Chapter 5 for buying information).

For portion sizes follow the instructions below. Vary the types of meat and vegetables you use.

That's it.

The rest of this chapter contains supplementary information, tips and various refinements but the simple diet described above is difficult to improve upon.

Do all dogs thrive on a natural diet?

With only a very, very few exceptions all dogs thrive on raw food.

Indeed, the only dogs that shouldn't eat a 100% natural diet are those with a compromised immune system or that have recently had bowel surgery.

What's more, a well-planned raw diet can really help dogs with health issues. If you would like to know more about how raw food can benefit a poorly dog see Chapter 12.

Remember, too, that Honey's Chief Veterinary Surgeon is available to supply dietary advice, free of charge and without any obligation on your part.

What dogs need from their food and how they get it

Food has two core functions. It provides energy and it helps the body to remain healthy.

With regard to energy the amount required will depend on a variety of circumstances, including how old the dog is (growing dogs need more, elderly dogs less), the amount of exercise being taken, whether the dog is pregnant or feeding puppies and the temperature (weirdly, dogs in really hot climates can need more energy as panting uses up more calories than you would imagine).

Interestingly, dogs do not need a lot of carbohydrates or simple sugars for energy (although a small amount of complex carbohydrate can provide useful fibre), as they can't digest it.

Their core dietary requirements are fat (it provides energy and protection and it enables the body to absorb fat-soluble vitamins), essential fatty acids (Omega 6 and Omega 3), protein (with essential amino acids) and a wide range of minerals and vitamins.

What a dog needs for energy is obtainable in its natural diet. All processed dog food companies are trying to do is replace what dogs ought to be eating with low-quality, inadequate, adulterated and inappropriate ingredients.

Suitable raw ingredients to feed your dog

Below is a list of all the different things you can feed your dog. An asterix (★) means that this is vital to your dog's health. The other ingredients are more by way of providing additional nutrition.

- **Lean muscle meat★**
  Chicken, beef, lamb, venison, rabbit, turkey, pork &c. Can be minced or diced.

- **Internal organs★**
  Heart, lung, liver, tripe &c. Liver should never be more than 10% of the total diet. Don't feed beef liver where the animal has been fed rape.

- **Fish**
  Any fish but especially fatty fish such as herring, salmon, pilchards and sardines. If you can't find fresh fish then once or twice a week you may like to add a tin of pilchards or herrings to the food.

- **Dairy**
  Cheese, probiotic yoghurt, goat's milk and/or small amounts of cottage cheese.

- **Eggs**
  Any type of whole egg, as an egg two or three times a week is an excellent source of protein, vitamins and omegas.

- **Bones★**
  Ideally raw, meaty bones and including chicken/turkey carcasses.

- **Leafy vegetables★**
  Spinach, winter greens, broccoli, cauliflower &c.

- **Root vegetables★**
  Carrots, parsnips, swede, turnips &c. but not potatoes, which are high in starch.

- **Fresh fruit**
  But not grapes or avocados and be sparing with dried fruits as they have a high sugar content.

- **Vegetable extracts**
  Brewer's yeast, kelp and/or a modest quantity of molasses.

- **Extra oil★**
  Once or twice a week you may care to add some cod liver, safflower, hemp, flax seed or sunflower oil.

You will notice that we are vague on the amount of, say, cod liver oil to add. Use your own judgement. For a small dog a teaspoonful will be enough, whereas for a really large dog you may like to add a tablespoonful.

Some useful tips

- The easiest way to meet your dog's nutritional needs is to serve them meat, offal and vegetables in their bowl and give them raw, meaty bones on the side.

- There is no magic proportion when it comes to the percentage of meat, offal and vegetable. I recommend ⅔ meat and offal and ⅓ vegetable. Others will suggest that 90% meat and offal is better, with just 10% vegetable. Treat dogs as individuals and take their likes and dislikes into account.

- Any raw meat will do – beef, lamb, pork, chicken, rabbit, venison, tripe, squirrel – anything, in fact, so long as it comes from a reputable source.

- Grate in the vegetable or put it through your food mixer. Any vegetables will do, but not raw potatoes.

- Vegetables should always be fresh. Vegetables really begin to lose their nutritional value a week or so after they have been picked.

- Mix the ingredients up well, as some dogs have a small child's aversion to vegetables.

- Don't forget to buy your dog raw, meaty bones. These contain vital nutrients, ensure healthy teeth and keep their stools firm.

- If you are going to make your food up yourself, you will probably find it saves you a lot of time to prepare a decent supply in advance and freeze it. One good way to do this is to shape it into rough patties or hamburgers.

What to say to your butcher

It is definitely worth finding a good butcher as it will save you a great deal of time and money. Also, if you live anywhere near a slaughterhouse then it is well worth seeing if they can supply you.

Either way, it is much, much easier if you have plenty of freezer space.

When searching for a butcher, explain what you are doing and ask for:

- scraps
- mince (this should be 'visually lean')
- inexpensive cuts
- offal (heart, kidneys and liver)
- green tripe (see below)
- raw, meaty bones
- chicken and other carcasses.

With regard to the scraps and the mince, it is fine for it to have some fat in it, but it shouldn't be too fatty (more than 30% fat would be a problem).

So far as inexpensive cuts are concerned, every butcher has his own ideas what these might be. Take 'skirt', which is the diaphragm under the ribs. Some butchers sell this for next to nothing; others know that there is good, lean meat to be had there and charge quite a bit for it. An efficient butcher will find you inexpensive ways to feed your dog.

See Chapter 5 for more information about buying bones.

Note that raw chicken carcasses and 'backs' are perfect for dogs and some people feed their dogs almost nothing else. Chicken wings are also great, a perfect parcel of meat and bone.

Some people feel it is important that the meat they buy for their dogs is suitable for human consumption. Others don't. The truth is that the dogs are unlikely to mind if it is a bit smelly and you shouldn't be too obsessed with the 'best before' date.

If you are looking for a convenient supply of ethically sourced meat and bones try Honey's Real Dog Food: www.honeysrealdogfood.com.

How much to serve

To begin with, you will need to monitor the quantity of food quite closely but once you get the hang of it, providing your dog is about the correct weight and looks fit, you can do it by feel. Lots of successful raw feeders simply watch their dogs carefully and adjust the quantity as they go.

There is no hard-and-fast rule but for a dog over 10kg roughly 2% of their body weight in food (including edible bones) every day should be about right. In other words, a 20kg dog should be eating roughly 400g. If you have a working dog, an underweight dog or a dog that exercises a great deal then up this amount to between 2% and 5% of body weight per day. If you have an elderly or overweight dog then reduce the amount to between 1% and 2% of bodyweight per day. You can serve it in as many meals as you want and at whatever time, but it should never be left down for the dog to eat when he or she feels like it. You might be interested to know that because wolves exercise so much they need about three times as much food as a typical dog.

For dogs under 11kg in weight try:

- 1–2kg: 10% of bodyweight
- 3–4kg: 7% of bodyweight
- 5–8kg: 5% of bodyweight
- 9–10kg: 3% of bodyweight
- 11kg+: 2% of bodyweight

If you would like more detailed advice please get in touch with Honey's. These percentages are for guidance only.

How to tell if your dog is the correct weight

The easiest way to tell if your adult dog is the right weight is to make sure that your dog's ribs are easily noticeable. Of course, for a hairy dog this isn't so easy! In this case run your hands over the rib cage. If it is easily felt, your dog is the right weight. If there is any fat… he or she needs to go on a bit of a diet!

A word about the 'RECOMMENDED DAILY INTAKE' figures

Dog food labelling makes great play of the 'recommended daily intake' figures for individual ingredients. Even some raw feeding experts refer to these so-called recommendations. By and large you can ignore them completely. They have almost no basis in fact. In America, for instance, the Association of American Feed Control Officials (AAFCO) and the US Food and Drug Administration (USFDA) have laid down figures based on 'the assumption that the animal should be able to survive on those quantities, with no observable ill effects for at least 3–6 months'.

Hardly meaningful. And, anyway, the actual recommendations change frequently as a result of pressure from dog food manufacturers.

The pros and cons of green tripe

If there were only one ingredient you could feed your dog, it would have to be green tripe. Nothing else offers such a variety of digestible proteins and your dog would thrive if fed nothing else. What is it? The dictionary defines it as: 'the raw, unbleached stomach of cattle or other ruminants, after no other treatment than a simple rinse in cold water'. It is called green because it has a green, fluorescent shine to it, although in colour it tends to be anything from light brown to black.

From a dog's perspective it is almost a wonder food, but from a human's perspective it has a couple of potential drawbacks.

To begin with, it contains a great deal of bacteria, some of which may be harmful to humans (but not dogs). For this reason, it can't be kept in the same fridge or freezer as food for human consumption. It must be handled and served carefully so that no contamination occurs. If you have any cuts or grazes on your skin you shouldn't touch it as it can lead to infection.

Then there is the smell. This is not only strong but also lingers. It's not a bad smell when you get used to it, but it's a devil to wash off and so it really is best to handle tripe using rubber gloves.

In short, it is a nuisance to deal with but well worth the effort if you can be bothered, especially as it is relatively inexpensive.

One final point, bleached tripe is worse than useless as the bleaching process strips out most of the goodness and leaves a potentially harmful chemical residue. Tripe that has been washed in plain water is not as good as green tripe but a less bothersome alternative and 100% safe for human handling.

Reassurance about parasites

The major dog food manufacturers clearly feel threatened by the natural feeding movement and there is definitely a campaign to discredit raw feeding. As part of this campaign it is sometimes suggested that there are dangerous parasites in raw meat. This is incorrect.

The main reason why you don't have to be afraid of parasites in a 'prey' animal being transferred to a 'predator' is that if this happened all predators would have become extinct long ago! Wolves simply wouldn't have survived. Also, one has to remember that, in the wild, carnivores frequently target sick and old animals as they are easier to catch and kill. So, not only is it safe for wolves to eat raw meat, but it is safe for them to eat raw meat from poorly prey.

Another reason not to be concerned is the acidity in a wolf's (or dog's) stomach. This is so strong that no known organism can survive exposure.

The parasites that survive on a herbivore are, by and large, very different from the parasites that attack carnivores. There is one exception to this: tapeworm. These can be caught from fleas found on rabbits; so, if a dog eats a whole rabbit (as opposed to rabbit meat), there is a risk. This won't affect you, though, unless you are giving your dog whole rabbit carcasses.

Incidentally, there is a prejudice against pork, because in the distant past pigs used to carry a parasite called trichinosis. This parasite was eradicated in farmed pork in the UK (and Europe) in the 1960s. If you are still nervous about parasites freeze the meat down for at least 20 days.

Please don't support intensive farming

For the most part farm animals lead short, painful lives in appalling conditions. They are kept indoors, in tiny cages, mutilated and transported hundreds and even thousands of miles before being killed. Furthermore, the way they are slaughtered is invariably drawn out and cruel.

The photographs and imagery used by farmers, producers, food manufacturers, butchers, marketing boards and supermarkets create, by and large, entirely the wrong impression. Only a tiny percentage of farm animals lead relatively happy and natural existences.

Unless the meat you buy meets certain criteria, the chances are that it has been intensively reared. To buy it is to support cruelty to animals. Of course, it is cheaper than meat from compassionately farmed animals: having a conscience does cost a little bit extra. But if you love animals, it is money well spent. What's more, intensively reared meat is much more likely to be packed with harmful chemicals since intensively farmed animals are given many more drugs to keep them alive.

To ensure that the meat you are buying has not been intensively reared insist that:

- Chicken, pork and turkey are free range.
- Rabbit and venison are free range or wild.
- Lamb and beef have been grass fed or are free range.

If you are buying organic meat, providing it is properly certified, you can be confident that it has been reared with animal welfare in mind.

It is much better for the environment and less wasteful to buy British. It is insane to buy lamb from, say, New Zealand when we have our own here at home. Also, beware of labelling. Ridiculous EU rules allow businesses to buy chickens in, say, Thailand but by cunning means describe them as being British.

If you would like to learn more about intensive farming, you might like to contact: Compassion in World Farming (www. ciwf.org.uk), which was started by an ordinary British farmer; the World Society for the Protection of Animals (www.wspa.org. uk), a leading pressure group; and/or the Soil Association (www. soilassociation.org), the UK's leading campaigner for higher standards of animal welfare.

Why fasting is good for your dog's health

From start to finish it can take a dog anything up to 20 hours to digest a full meal, a full meal being the amount it can fit in its stomach at a single sitting. This is a very long time when compared to humans, who eat much smaller meals and digest them much faster. Why is the time it takes a dog to digest important? Because a dog's digestive system needs to rest for periods to operate at optimum efficiency. More than this, if the system doesn't get a chance to rest it can be harmful to the dog's health (it needs the time for its liver to transform fat to glucose). My advice is to feed your dog once a day, never to leave food down for it (eat it or lose it being the rule) and to fast your dog at least once a week.

Achieving balance

Dogs don't eat completely balanced meals in the wild, but get the nutrition they need over time. You don't, therefore, have to worry too much about balancing each meal you feed. Rather, you should be thinking about the balance over a week or even a month:

- The meat, organs and bones should account for no less than ⅔ of your dog's diet.
- Provide plenty of variety: it ensures your dog is getting all the nutrition it needs from different sources.
- Your dog shouldn't really need extra supplements, but if you decide to give them be sparing and watch for the effects.

Unless you have a dog with a serious health issue, there is no reason to worry about the exact nutritional value of each element of your dog's natural diet.

Storing, serving (and travelling with) raw food

You will find that most natural feeders depend upon freezers to make their lives easier as it is a nuisance having to buy fresh ingredients every few days. The easiest approach is to make up a batch of food, divide it into daily portions, freeze them all and then thaw as needed. The freezing process does nothing to reduce the nutritional value of the food and it is absolutely fine to freeze bones and carcasses.

Food should be thawed before serving. It is better not to use a microwave to thaw food. Microwaves work by concentrating heat on selected spots within the food. These spots will be considerably hotter (and thus more damaging to health) than if you simply cooked the food. If you need to thaw food quickly, put it in a plastic bag and run cold water over it.

There is no health risk associated with freezing food, thawing or partly thawing it, and then freezing it again. This is because modern domestic freezers are so efficient that they bring the food down to minus 18 degrees – quite cold enough to kill off any dangerous bacteria. What does happen is that food repeatedly frozen and thawed becomes increasingly mushy and bloody.

Going on holiday is always a bit of a challenge to natural feeders.

If you don't have access to a freezer, the best option is to take the food frozen and to keep it as cold as possible. It doesn't actually matter if the meat is a little smelly when served (your dog won't mind!) but after a few days the vegetable element will start to lose its nutritional value. Still, with careful management food should last for up to nine days in a fridge.

A word about hygiene

Dogs may have stomach acids so strong that they would burn your fingers, but humans don't. Raw food does have bacteria on it that could cause health issues for humans. Keep it separate from the food you are going to eat, thoroughly wash any surface it comes into contact with (including utensils, storage containers and so forth) as well as your hands. Use an anti-bacterial soap or mild disinfectant and/or wear rubber gloves. If you don't want to use harmful chemicals, vinegar is a natural alternative.

10.
MAKING THE SWITCH

TEN

The vast majority of dogs make the switch from processed food to raw food with no problem whatsoever and, generally speaking, the best approach is to fast your dog for a day and then to start them on their new, natural diet.

Troubleshooting tips

So, what problems might you encounter?

The most common issue when switching is that the dog turns its nose up at the raw food and refuses to eat it. If this happens, don't worry! Remember, a dog can go up to a week without food and be none the worse for it. Give your dog a single chance to eat every 24 hours, and if he or she doesn't pounce on it with enthusiasm the moment you put the bowl down, lift it straight back up and wait another day. It is not a good idea to ever leave food down for your dog. If you are too soft-hearted for this approach, try one of the switching options mentioned below.

(You may be interested to know that really intelligent dogs from loving homes are more likely to refuse raw food. Why? Their hunger for attention is greater than their hunger for food. Being smart, they realise that if they don't eat you'll make a fuss of them and this makes them happier than anything else can.)

Another problem can be regurgitation immediately after eating. This is almost certainly caused by a conditioned reflex. The dog's stomach is expecting the normal food and has prepared the wrong kind of enzymes to digest it. When the new food turns up, the system rejects it. It is quite normal in nature for a dog to eat something, vomit it up and eat it again. It is, of course, up to you whether you allow this. But you shouldn't panic. The solution to this sort of vomiting is, initially, patience and then to use one of the switching options mentioned below. Incidentally, dogs may also vomit bones because they aren't used to eating them, and some people suspect that dogs vomit a meal that they really enjoyed eating so that they can have the pleasure of eating it again! If you have been raw feeding for a couple of weeks and the dog suddenly vomits, this may be an attempt to rid the body of toxins and is not unusual. *Obviously, if your dog is vomiting frequently you should check with your vet that there isn't any serious underlying health problem.*

You shouldn't panic, either, if your dog's stools are runny. It is probably caused by the change in diet and will pass in a few days. It could also be the result of not enough bone in the diet as it is the bone that tends to make the stools firmer. The solution to runny stools is, initially, patience and then to use one of the switching options mentioned below or the remedies in Chapter 12. You could also increase the bone element of the dog's diet.

If your dog seems to have a problem with a particular ingredient try it for two or three days and then drop it and come back to it later.

Switching options

The easiest option is to fast the dog and just make the switch, as described above. The only reason to try another approach is if you encounter some problem making a direct switch. Here are the other options:

Tripe

Fast for a day and then make the switch immediately, but only feed your dog green tripe to begin with. Dogs find this incredibly easy to digest and it contains all the nutrients they need. (For more information about tripe, see the previous chapter.)

Mixing

Slowly start adding raw food to whatever it is you normally feed, increasing the amount every day until it is 100% raw after one or two weeks. This gives the dog's stomach time to adjust to the change. If the dog is vomiting then, having checked it isn't a medical issue, extend the period over which you make the switch. It doesn't really matter if it takes a month or more.

Cooking

Take the raw food and cook it in a pan (not a microwave and not the bones). Every day cook it slightly less until it is raw. This gives the dog's stomach time to adjust to the change from sterile, processed food.

Dogs and vegetables

Some dogs love vegetables; others don't, and the ones who don't may decline to eat their food for this reason. The solution? Give in to them! Remove vegetable from their diet completely and wait for a week or two before gradually reintroducing it. Another approach is to pour a little real gravy or break an egg over the food before serving it, as this will disguise the taste.

What to do if your dog becomes too thin

If your dog loses an unnatural amount of weight after switching to a natural diet, it will usually be because:

- The dog isn't receiving enough food and/or the food being provided has too low a fat content. The solution is to increase the amount of food and/or the fat content.

- The dog's stomach has not yet learnt to digest the raw food (bear in mind that it will need extra elasticity and muscle power). This is likely to be the problem if the dog is producing a large amount of waste matter. The solution is to try one of the switching techniques described elsewhere in this chapter.

Three things to watch out for

There are three possible issues that you should watch out for during the switchover period.

Bloat

One extremely rare condition to watch out for when switching your dog to a raw food diet is bloat. Bloat is caused by the stomach twisting so that food can't pass between the oesophagus and the intestine. When this happens, the digestion process comes to a halt, the food will become subject to bacterial growth and gases will build up, forcing the stomach to look like a balloon. The risk of bloat is higher for large breeds and for dogs that have only been fed many small meals all their lives and then suddenly get to eat too much, with no rest afterwards. Also dogs that over-exercise after eating. If you think your dog may have bloat, contact your vet immediately.

Yellow bile

If your dog's stool contains yellow bile for several days running after the introduction of raw food, it may indicate a pancreatic problem. This isn't caused by raw food; rather, it is revealed by it. You should talk to your vet about this problem.

Itchy 'hot' spots

Itchy hot spots suggest that the food you are providing is a little too rich in one or more specific proteins. Vary the protein source (switch to different meats) or increase the fat and/or vegetable content.

The difference between runny stools and diarrhoea

There is a huge difference between soft or runny stools and diarrhoea.

It is normal, when switching diet, for dogs to experience soft or runny stools and it can occur if they aren't eating enough bone.

True diarrhoea is virtually liquid – like soup.

A reliable remedy (apart from increasing the amount of bone you are feeding) is to give the dog slippery elm. Some people recommend mashed boiled sweet potato and leek to firm up stools. There are other remedies mentioned in Chapter 12. If you are worried, return the dog to the old diet and start again when things have settled down.

At what point do you call in a vet? In the case of runny stools don't wait more than a week. In the case of true diarrhoea you probably shouldn't delay more than 24 hours.

Incidentally, true diarrhoea is not caused by raw food per se but will almost certainly be the result of either a parasite or gastrointestinal problem. If the latter, all that has happened is that the raw feeding has exposed the underlying problem.

When to seek experienced help

There are circumstances when a switch to raw feeding should only be undertaken with experienced guidance. Dogs that have recently undergone bowel surgery or chemotherapy or that have a compromised immune system can all benefit from a natural diet but may need a special diet. Also, pregnant dogs and new mums will have special nutritional needs. Please do contact us at Honey's for free advice (you don't have to be a customer) or consult a vet or other professional with raw feeding expertise.

11.
A FEEDING PLAN FOR
MUMS AND PUPPIES

ELEVEN

Bitches fed on a well-balanced, raw food diet are more fertile, enjoy easier pregnancies and produce healthier puppies. The puppies themselves, if raised on raw food, grow into healthier dogs and lead longer lives. This is because a well-balanced, raw food diet is what dogs are biologically designed to eat.

We don't have to look far to see why. Imagine feeding generation upon generation of humans on an inadequate diet. We know from what happens in developing nations (and to the disadvantaged in Western countries) that a poor diet leads to lower fertility, bad health and shorter life expectancy, whereas humans that eat what nature intended enjoy higher fertility, better health and longer life expectancy. Dogs are no different. They need the diet that nature intended – raw meat, raw bones and a certain amount of vegetable matter – to achieve optimum health.

Diet and so-called genetic conditions

Much has been said in the media and elsewhere about how overbreeding has caused all sorts of genetic health conditions in dogs. While this is true, it diverts attention from another possible cause.

Processed food has two serious drawbacks. First, it is seriously deficient in the ingredients dogs need to maintain good health. Second, it contains ingredients that actually damage a dog's health. When experts describe a health issue as being 'genetic', they may be overlooking something more obvious: the effect of feeding processed food to generation upon generation of dogs.

A good example of this is skeletal disease. Almost unheard of before processed food, bone disease is now widespread in the West.

For dogs to have healthy bones they need the calcium and other vital bone-building nutrients that are only found in raw bones. Each generation that doesn't receive these vital bone-building nutrients is weaker than the last. Modern solutions to bone disease, involving various treatments as well as culling and selective breeding, are never going to solve the problem. What has to happen is a re-building of healthy 'stock' by means of the correct diet.

Natural feeding for mums and expectant mums

Mums and expectant mums require more food than other adult dogs. Apart from this, there is no difference in the way they should be fed. However, there are certain extra ingredients and supplements you may like to consider.

Before you start

Just before your mum-to-be (hopefully) comes into season you should start to increase, very slightly, the amount of nutrition she receives. Reduce the amount of vegetable in her diet and give her more chicken wings and more eggs. If you are concerned that she may have trouble conceiving, you could consider some extra supplements, such as cod liver oil, vitamin E, multi B, vitamin C and foods high in zinc. Don't add supplements without taking professional advice.

Be careful about foods (especially commercial foods) supplemented with glucosamine, as this can interfere with conception. You want her to be increasing in weight as she comes to be mated because her body will respond to the increase in nutrition by increasing her hormone production. This in turn leads to greater fertility. You should carry on feeding her a little more than usual for about a week after mating and then drop back to the normal amount.

Incidentally, check that the mum isn't anaemic (a sure sign of a poor diet) and make sure that she is free of any external parasites (fleas and ear mites) as well as internal parasites (intestinal worms and heartworm). The mum should be at her ideal weight, that is to say slim without being too thin. She should have lots of energy, a pliant elastic skin, a shiny coat, a light covering of fat and well-developed muscles.

Once she has conceived

If mum is on a raw food diet then for the first two-thirds of her pregnancy, unless she has some health issue that needs addressing, there is probably no requirement to alter her normal feeding routine. In the last third of her term, that is to say the last three weeks, you should aim to gradually increase the amount of food. This is because the puppies do most of their growing during this period.

The general rule is:

- Week 6: increase by 5–10%
- Week 7: increase by another 5–10%
- Week 8: increase by another 5–10%

By the time she reaches the end of the eighth week, she should be eating around a third to a half as much as her normal diet. Incidentally, don't feed it all to her in one sitting but spread it over the day and be mindful of her general condition.

- Week 9: start reducing the amount of food very slightly

By the time she has the puppies she should be eating about a quarter of what she was eating in week eight. She should be eating less bone and more vegetables, as you want her diet to have a gentle laxative effect. On the day before giving birth, many mums go off their food completely.

Mum may be eating more in those last few weeks, but she shouldn't be getting fat. What she needs is extra protein, vitamins, essential fatty acids and minerals, exactly what you will find in a well-balanced raw food diet. Incidentally, there are a couple of things you need to avoid during pregnancy.

First of all, don't give any food with too much Vitamin A (such as cod liver oil) in the first five or six weeks of the pregnancy, as it can be dangerous to foetal health. Before the pregnancy and once mum is lactating, cod liver oil is valuable, however. Second, don't give mum any extra calcium while she is pregnant. Indeed, in the last week or two many breeders switch to a lower-calcium diet. Why? Because this is what mums do in the wild! They eat much more meat (and organ meat, especially liver, which has a laxative effect) than bones. They want the higher protein. Too much calcium during pregnancy can cause tissue calcification and other birth defects in puppies.

After the happy day

If your new mum wants to eat the afterbirth then you shouldn't stop her. It is full of nutrients that will help to nourish her in the first few days after the puppies have been born when she may not feel like leaving the puppies or eating.

By and large if your new mum is on a well-balanced raw food diet then while she is feeding her puppies she can usually be given as much food as she feels like. The only time you might limit her intake would be during the first week or if the litter were very small. After the puppies are born, mum should return to close to her ideal weight, that is to say the weight she was before she became pregnant, and she should maintain this weight until the puppies are weaned. This will be over a five- to six-week period with the peak demands for milk in weeks three to five.

When you wean the puppies off their mother's milk, you should reduce the amount of food you are giving her. You want her body to register that milk is no longer required. Assuming that she is producing ample quantities of milk, cut her food back to the normal amount and stop giving her chicken wings until her milk has dried up.

How a natural diet boosts fertility

The first thing to remember is that it takes two to tango! Dogs are just as likely to suffer from fertility issues as bitches are. Most manufactured dog food offers a narrow spectrum of nutrients, damaged fats and proteins, high chemical and grain levels, high levels of artificial calcium, salt and sugar mixed with low levels of natural antioxidants, enzymes, available micronutrients and phytochemicals and… but you get the idea.

One of the effects of feeding processed food to several generations of dogs, according to Dr Ian Billinghurst in his book *Grow Your Pups with Bones*, is substantially reduced fertility. He points out that 'the best way to be certain of low to nonexistent fertility … is to feed dogs a dry food starting from when they are puppies'. Billinghurst then goes on to explain why the different elements (essential fatty acids, vitamin A, vitamin C, antioxidants and so forth) in a raw food diet boost fertility. For males he lays great stress on the need for zinc, which occurs naturally in lamb, beef, chicken, liver, eggs and carrots as well as methionine (found in eggs), magnesium (found in green vegetables), manganese (again found in green vegetables) and selenium (found in eggs). Billinghurst feels that it is always better for dogs to obtain all these nutrients from their food and warns against overdoing it with supplements. Where supplements may be required, it is vital to get professional advice as it is possible to overdose a dog on ingredients such as zinc.

How wolves feed their pups

For the first three or four weeks, puppies live on their mother's milk. Interestingly, if something happens to the mother then another bitch from the same pack will take over. Female wolves have the ability to produce milk even if they haven't given birth. The milk not only provides all the nourishment required but also helps to build each puppy's immunity to disease.

At around three to four weeks (and sometimes earlier) puppies will start to pick up food scraps discarded by the other wolves in the pack. They will play with the food and chew on it. In this way they learn to eat. Milk will be part of their diet until they are around seven weeks.

At around six to seven weeks the mother and other members of the pack will start regurgitating their own food and giving it to the puppies. Puppies may eat regurgitated food as part of their diet for up to 20 weeks after they are born.

The switch to adult food is gradual, usually starting at around 12 weeks and finishing at 16 weeks, which is about the time the puppies get their permanent teeth.

Feeding newborn puppies

It is vital to a dog's long-term health that he or she eat the best possible food when being weaned. It is especially damaging to puppies to allow them to eat processed foods containing harmful ingredients, additives and chemicals. A puppy's stomach lining is more permeable than an adult dog's, so the risk of causing lasting health issues is much greater.

For the first three weeks of their lives, your puppies need nothing more than their mother's milk. Weaning should be a gradual process starting at three to four weeks and finishing at about eight weeks, assuming that mum's milk holds out. If mum starts to dry up then you may need to speed things up a little. The earliest a puppy can really be started on solid food is 3 weeks of age. As with humans, the longer puppies drink (within an 8- to 12-week timeframe… not indefinitely!) their mother's milk, the better it is for their development.

At three weeks it is a good idea to offer puppies cut-up bits of chicken wing for them to lick and play with. It doesn't matter if they eat anything. You just want them to become familiar with the smell and taste.

You should slowly introduce solid food after the fourth week. After about six or seven weeks the puppies should be nearly weaned. They may still be drinking mum's milk, but it won't be their main source of nutrition. Incidentally, if there are foods you want your puppies to eat when they are adults this is a good time to introduce them.

In terms of volume of food there is no hard-and-fast rule but, generally speaking, you should follow these guidelines:

0–4 months:	8%
4–6 months:	6–8%
6–9 months:	4%
9–12 months:	3%
> 12 months:	2%

The percentage refers to the weight of the food to be fed per day in relation to the body weight of the puppy. So a puppy aged less than 4 months would receive 8% of its body weight every day.

The transition should be gradual, not sudden. So the day a puppy turns 6 months you don't suddenly drop the food from 8% to 4%, and in the case of miniature and smaller breeds you need to up the quantity by up to half as much again.

Do remember that no two dogs have the same metabolism and the above is for general guidance only. The precise ingredients of what you feed will also have a bearing on quantities.

Puppy feeding tips

Make the move from mother's milk to raw feeding gently. It takes a few weeks for a puppy's digestive system to cope with a 100% adult diet.

There is an argument for feeding puppies the more solid food in the evening as this gives them time to digest the food properly while they are sleeping.

During the transition, you might like to give your puppies foods that are easy to digest such as egg yolks, natural yoghurt, goat's milk and even a bit of mashed-up vegetable. In weeks four, five and six you could offer lightly cooked chicken and perhaps add some probiotic and digestive enzymes. Chicken wings are fine from six weeks but ideally should be from young birds. Puppies shouldn't be given any food with more than a 10% or 15% bone content until after they are 10 or 12 weeks old.

Remember that, in the wild, puppies would be eating the

regurgitated, semi-digested contents of their mother's stomach. These easy-to-digest foods are in addition to the more 'solid' raw food you will be providing.

Feed your puppy three or four times a day up until the age of 12 weeks and then twice a day until fully grown. Small breeds tend to reach full size at between 8 and 10 months, larger breeds from between 10 months and a year. Giant breeds may take as long as 16 months to reach maturity.

Go easy on liver! It can cause runny stools. Lamb liver is best.

If possible, feed only organic ingredients. It is best to keep as many potentially harmful chemicals out of your puppy's system as possible.

You shouldn't really need to add supplements, but if you feel you want to then consider kelp powder, B vitamins, vitamin C, flax or hemp seed oil and even the occasional multivitamin pill. But approach supplements cautiously and seek professional advice. Note a little garlic and ginger in the diet will help to ward off parasites.

Puppy feeding plan

- 0–3 weeks: Mother's milk
- 3–4 weeks: Start on soft foods such as egg yolks, lightly cooked chicken, mashed-up vegetables. Let them play with 'adult food'. Three meals a day.
- 6 weeks: Introduce chicken wings and more adult food but not too much bone.
- 12 weeks: Full adult diet and cut back to two meals a day. Occasional fasting.
- Fully grown: One meal a day and regular fasting.

If your dog is pregnant or feeding puppies please don't hesitate to contact us for additional advice and information.

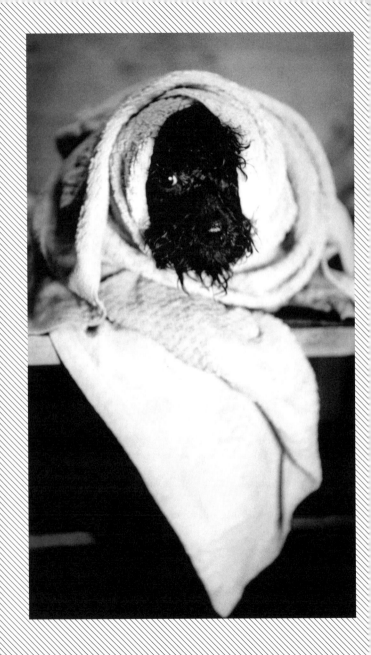

12.
NATURAL DIETS FOR SICK AND POORLY DOGS

WHAT YOU'LL FIND IN THIS CHAPTER

Conditions relating to the digestive system

- Bloat or gastric torsion
- Colitis
- Coprophagia (eating faeces)
- Constipation
- Diarrhoea
- Flatulence
- Inflammatory bowel disease
- Irritable bowel syndrome
- Vomiting
- Prebiotics and probiotics

Internal conditions

- Addison's disease
- Cushing's syndrome
- Diabetes mellitus
- Exocrine pancreatic insufficiency
- Hepatitis (liver disease)
- Impacted anal glands
- Kidney disease (renal failure)
- Liver shunt
- Pancreatitus
- Kidney stones and other purine problems

Oral conditions

- Gingivitis
- Halitosis (bad breath)

Skin conditions

- Alopecia (fur loss)
- Itchy skin
- Paw chewing
- Itchy ears and skin problems caused by allergies

Other conditions

- Arthritis
- Cancers and tumours
- Dicospondylitis
- Elbow dysplasia
- Epilepsy
- Hip dysplasia
- Lafora
- Luxating patella
- Osteochrondritis dissecans
- Spondylosis
- Von Willebrand disease
- A word about steroids

TWELVE

There is an extremely close connection between diet and health. Eating the wrong foods can cause all sorts of medical issues, whereas eating the right foods can do much to alleviate (and even cure) a wide range of conditions.

In this chapter you will find a short description of some of the most frequently found canine medical conditions, together with advice on what food, herbs and supplements to give to sufferers.

As Hippocrates said: 'Let food be your medicine.'

Mostly raw

With one or two exceptions (primarily where the dog's immune system has been compromised), you will see that a raw food diet is always recommended. This is because raw food is the easiest thing for your dog to digest and supports his or her immune system. Where raw feeding isn't recommended, you should not revert to processed food but simply cook the ingredients in the way prescribed. Processed food is an underlying cause for as many as 9 out of 10 visits to the vet, and this includes expensive, so-called scientifically developed, brands.

The importance of pure, clean water

Water is treated with a great number of chemicals. Ill dogs are less tolerant of these chemicals, and so it is advisable to find a source of pure, clean water. This could be a mineral water (better from a glass bottle than plastic as plastic bottles left in the sun alter the chemical composition of their contents), rainwater or filtered water.

Why ill dogs do better on organic food

Intensively reared meat and intensively farmed vegetables, especially those imported from developing nations, are likely to contain a surprisingly high percentage of unnatural chemicals (everything from growth hormones to nitrates and from steroids to pesticides). Furthermore, meat will include the residue of whatever the animal has been fed. This is particularly relevant in the case of grain-fed livestock and poultry, and grain is especially harmful to dogs. It is better, therefore, to feed organic food to ill dogs.

Free dietary advice

If you need dietary advice, don't forget it is available, free of charge and without obligation, from Honey's Real Dog Food. See the back cover for contact information.

CONDITIONS RELATING TO THE DIGESTIVE SYSTEM

Bloat or gastric torsion

Since the 1980s, the incidence of bloat (also known as gastric torsion, gastric dilatation-volvulus, or GDV) has increased dramatically. In this condition the stomach twists or flips over on itself and air is trapped. Then any food in the stomach begins to ferment, creating further gases. Later on, circulation to the stomach and spleen are cut off to the point where the dog may go into shock and die. It seems to affect mature, deep-chested dogs the most, especially larger breeds. The condition is extremely serious and potentially fatal. If you suspect bloat, contact your vet immediately.

For a dog that has suffered and survived bloat, a dry food or kibble diet is definitely not to be recommended. Instead, switch the dog to a raw food diet, which has been shown to improve the chances of preventing a recurrence. After bloat, many dogs lose weight and it is important to get this back on as soon as possible, since a healthy weight is one of the factors that reduce risk. Having said this, too much fat in the diet can be harmful. Instead, use lean meat and increase the frequency of meals and total volume of food served. One of the best things to give dogs that have suffered bloat is green tripe. Avoid vegetables as the fermentation process can produce gas.

It is still not entirely clear why so many dogs appear to be getting bloat. One theory is that dry food is the cause. Most cases seem to occur quite late at night (between 9 p.m. and 2 a.m.). Bloat may be related to stress of some type. Interestingly, dogs that appear to be happy are much less prone to this condition.

Colitis

Colitis is either acute or chronic inflammation of the colon and the symptoms aren't terribly pleasant. In acute cases expect vomiting, with diarrhoea containing mucous and blood. In chronic cases the dog will frequently try to pass watery, blood-streaked, mucous and putrid stools. The dog may suffer from flatulence and vomiting. There may be weight loss over time. Do not, however, panic when your vet diagnoses colitis, as it is the cause of around half the cases of diarrhoea in dogs and is relatively common and very treatable.

What causes it? Generally speaking, it is the result of eating something unsuitable (perhaps picked up while on a walk), food intolerances or allergies. Other causes can include infection or parasites. Some cases may be stressed-related, and there is a possibility of an autoimmune cause.

In terms of treatment there is every reason to continue raw feeding since this is the easiest food for your dog to digest. If there is the possibility of a compromised immune system, lightly cook the meat before serving. Avoid gluten (grains) and dairy products. Use both a prebiotic and a probiotic. A period of fasting may be appropriate.

Constipation

Constipation can occur if a dog becomes dehydrated or has too much bone in his or her diet without sufficient fibre. Other rare causes can be too little magnesium and/or too much aluminium in the dog's diet and also nerve degeneration. One of the benefits of a natural diet is that your dog is less likely to become constipated, but if it does become a problem then add more soluble fibre (ripe apple, pears or tinned sardines or pilchards), while cutting back on the bone element. Reduce the number of chicken wings given, if relevant. Incorporating liver or offal into the diet once or twice a week can help.

Coprophagia (eating faeces)

Human beings may find coprophagia (the medical term for eating excrement) disgusting, but to a dog it is a perfectly normal part of their diet. It is believed to have various causes:

1. The artificial flavouring and appetite stimulants in processed food frequently pass straight through the digestive system without being absorbed into the body. As a result this can give dog (and cat) faeces a very attractive flavour. It is worth noting that dogs fed pineapple sometimes produce less appealing excrement.

2. Boredom! This is especially true in the case of younger dogs and those in kennels who may not have enough to occupy them. Regular exercise, companionship and a selection of toys may help.

3. A mineral or trace element may be lacking from the diet. Adding offal (liver or kidney) to the dog's diet may provide the missing nutrients. A broad-spectrum supplement for trace minerals such as Dorwest Keeper's Mix may also be of value.

4. The intestinal flora may be out of balance, possibly as a result of a course of antibiotics. This is especially true if dogs are eating bovine and equine faeces (cow and horse poo, in plain English). A course of prebiotics and probiotics is recommended.

5. Submissive behaviour within a pack. Less senior members of a pack will eat the Alpha dog's faeces as an ingratiating behaviour. This is a harder problem to solve. A homeopathic remedy may be of great assistance.

Coprophagia can also lead to worms. Worms can also lead to coprophagia. Therefore, treatment against worms is advisable.

Diarrhoea

There is a huge difference between soft or runny stools and diarrhoea. There is rarely any need to be concerned about soft or runny stools. Diarrhoea, when switching to a raw diet, is also not uncommon for the first few days. True diarrhoea is virtually liquid (like soup) and movements are frequent. There are lots of different reasons for diarrhoea, including:

*   bacterial infection such as salmonella, E. coli, clostridia and campylobacter
*   fungal infection
*   viral infection such as parvovirus, distemper and coronavirus
*   yeast infection such as *Candida albicans*
*   parasites such as worms, coccidia and protozoa
*   poison
*   tumours
*   stress
*   malabsorption syndromes.

It is obviously important to establish the cause before treatment can be recommended, and to this end it may be necessary to run blood and/or faeces tests. Depending on the seriousness of the condition, the options are to (a) do nothing, (b) fast the dog for 24 hours and (c) ask your vet for advice.

If it continues for more than 24 hours you should consult a vet.

Tips for dealing with runny stools and diarrhoea:

1. Feed a natural diet and plenty of pure, clean water.
2. Give some prebiotics (see below) to feed the good bacteria in the stomach.
3. Use a probiotic (but ideally not live yoghurt). See below for details.
4. Try to avoid antibiotics, steroids and anti-inflammatory drugs unless the dog is seriously ill.
5. Try slippery elm or a modest amount of brewer's yeast to aid digestion.
6. Psyllium husk can be added to thicken the stools.
7. Try a remedy such as Ferrum Phosphoricum 12× or 6× tissue salt to help slow the diarrhoea and increase absorption.

Please note that gluten, cereals, cereal by products and modified starch all contribute to canine digestive problems.

Flatulence

All dogs, regardless of their diet, are likely to have a certain amount of flatulence. The most frequent cause is the carbohydrates in processed food – easily remedied by a switch to natural feeding. Antibiotics may also be responsible, in which case a course of probiotics will often help. A small percentage of dogs produce wind as a result of eating vegetables, or particular vegetables, and this can be dealt with by reducing the percentage of vegetables being served or excluding them completely. Incorporating more chicken wings in the diet can help, and so can adding a human-grade organic bone meal supplement.

Inflammatory bowel disease

Inflammatory bowel disease (IBD) is a relatively new condition in dogs and similar to Crohn's disease in humans. It is a chronic inflammatory intestinal disease that can occur anywhere in the digestive tract, but most commonly involves the small intestine and colon.

What should you watch out for? Recurrent bouts of diarrhoea, that is sometimes watery, explosive, odd-coloured (yellowish), mucous-coated, slimy and often has blood streaks. Vomiting (sometimes blood-tinged) is not unusual and the dog may have abdominal pain with distension to the bowel and abdomen. The stomach may emit gurgling noises. Dogs are often lethargic with weight loss and may have an increase or loss of appetite. As these symptoms are similar to other conditions it can be difficult to make a positive diagnosis.

In terms of treatment there is every reason to continue raw feeding, since this is the easiest food for your dog to digest. However, reduce the fat content, avoid all grains and dairy products and increase the amount of fibre, such as psyllium husk. Slippery elm can help, too. Use both a prebiotic and a probiotic.

Irritable bowel syndrome

Irritable bowel syndrome (IBS) is difficult to diagnose because so many of the symptoms, which may be intermittent, are shared with other conditions. You should watch out for intermittent bouts of diarrhoea or soft stools, increased frequency of defecation, small stools, straining to defecate, abdominal distension (bloating), flatulence, weight loss and, sometimes, vomiting. The stomach may emit gurgling noises. It is believed that diet and stress are the main causes, with some drugs aggravating an already sensitive digestive system.

In terms of treatment there is every reason to continue raw feeding since this is the easiest food for your dog to digest. If there is the possibility of a compromised immune system then lightly cook the food before serving. Avoid gluten (grains) and dairy products. Use both a prebiotic and a probiotic. Slippery elm can be a great help.

Vomiting

It is important to remember that dogs regularly regurgitate their food, and this process should not be confused with vomiting that is due to a potential or underlying health issue.

If a dog vomits repeatedly and/or seems unwell in other ways then it warrants contacting a vet. However, if the dog isn't vomiting repeatedly and has no other apparent symptoms, you may like to start by fasting him or her for 24 hours, ensuring that there is an ample supply of pure, clean water available throughout. If your dog seems to be over drinking or having trouble keeping water down then give him or her a block of ice, which will thaw slowly ensuring a constant but reduced supply of water.

Assuming the dog has stopped vomiting after 24 hours, offer a small, light meal. This can consist of scrambled egg or cooked chicken with a prebiotic and a probiotic. If vomiting doesn't reoccur then towards the end of the second day serve a smaller-than-usual meal of whatever the dog normally eats. Resume your ordinary schedule of feeding on day three.

Note: If vomiting continues or is constant or if it contains blood or if it is in tandem with diarrhoea, consult your vet immediately.

Prebiotics and probiotics

Dogs, like human beings, have bacteria living in their gut. The bacteria themselves are made up of 'unfriendly' strains that can make the dog ill and 'friendly' strains that keep it well. Normally, the balance is in favour of the 'friendly' bacteria, but sometimes – such as after a course of antibiotics, during stress or through poor diet – the 'unfriendly' bacteria get the upper hand. This is called intestinal dysbiosis, a bacterial imbalance that results in an overgrowth of bad bacteria and yeast. Dysbiosis has been linked to various disorders, including yeast infections, irritable bowel syndrome and rheumatoid arthritis. It is treated by restoring the balance with prebiotics, probiotics and a healthy (natural) diet.

Probiotics are beneficial bacteria that can be found in various foods. When you eat probiotics, you will add these healthy bacteria to your intestinal tract. Common strains include the *Lactobacillus* and *Bifidobacterium* families of bacteria. Prebiotics, on the other hand, are non-digestible foods that make their way through our digestive system and help good bacteria grow and flourish. Prebiotics keep beneficial bacteria healthy.

Happily, you don't need to buy special canine prebiotics or probiotics, as those designed for humans work perfectly. If you need a prebiotic, try aloe vera. If you need a probiotic, try one containing *Lactobacillus*, *Acidophilus* and/or *Bifidus*-type bacteria with FOS (fructooligosaccharides). Use the minimum recommended human dose. Prebiotics include aloe vera and chicory.

INTERNAL CONDITIONS

Addison's disease

Addison's disease is the opposite of Cushing's syndrome in as much that the adrenal gland does not produce enough corticosteroid. It can be a side effect of the drugs used to treat Cushing's. It is less common than Cushing's and can lead to other health issues.

The adrenal gland secretes several substances that help regulate normal bodily functions. Some of the most important products are glucocorticoids and mineralocorticoids. Glucocorticoids such as cortisol have an effect on sugar, fat and protein metabolism. Mineralocorticoids such as aldosterone help to regulate blood pressure and allow the kidneys to maintain a proper water–salt balance in the body (by helping the kidneys retain sodium and excrete potassium). If the adrenal glands are not functioning properly, and the production level of aldosterone drops, a drop in blood pressure and severe dehydration can occur. Dysfunctioning adrenal glands are the main cause of Addison's disease.

Symptoms include muscle weakness and general lethargy, diarrhoea and vomiting, hyperpigmentation, joint pain, lack of appetite and muscle shivers and tremors. The usual treatment is hormone replacement with drugs such as fludrocortisone.

Diet should be under veterinary supervision. Changes in the health of the patient may require a change of diet and this will only be known if blood is monitored. Avoid vegetables and other foods high in vitamin A (such as carrots, celery and liver), also foods high in potassium (bananas, most meats but especially pork). Raw chicken or turkey are excellent as they have low potassium levels. Salt will generally have to be added to the diet, but this will depend on the blood analysis. Fresh adrenal gland in the diet can be beneficial as can dehydrated adrenal gland as a supplement. It is important that the patient is not stressed. Some herbal and homeopathic remedies can help to achieve this. Patients may also benefit from a small amount of quinoa or porridge - as well as chia seeds, cottage cheese, tuna, egg, sunflower or pumpkin seeds, raw walnuts and raw almonds. The most important thing is to stabilise salt levels and maintain sodium levels.

Cushing's syndrome

Cushing's syndrome is an enlargement of the adrenal glands resulting in increased production of adrenocortical hormones. Symptoms increase thirst, appetite and the need to urinate. With time the dog can develop a potbelly and an intolerance to exercise with some cases showing muscle spasms and difficulty bending their legs. The coat becomes dry, hairs fine and the skin thins. Hair loss around the flanks and abdomen can spread to the legs, back and head.

The diet has to be easy on the liver and help the thyroid gland. High-fat diets should be avoided and the best recipes to follow are chicken with some offal, rabbit and chicken mixed together, venison or lean beef. In terms of vegetables carrot is excellent (for the beta carotene) and broccoli, garlic and grapefruit seed extract. The best supplement to help the thyroid is kelp or a similar seaweed. For the liver add milk thistle and for the heart (patients are likely to suffer from raised cholesterol) add hawthorn. The addition of fresh adrenal gland and/or dehydrated gland powder can also help stabilize these cases. The diet and supplements need to be changed radically should the patient slip from Cushing's to Addison's. Other supplements that will help patients with Cushing's include vitamins A and D (cod liver oil), vitamin B6, folic acid, vitamin C, vitamin K, calcium, magnesium, potassium, selenium, brewer's yeast and zinc. However, you should not add extra supplements to the diet without consulting a vet. Herbal and homeopathic vets have much to offer in the treatment.

Diabetes mellitus

Diabetes mellitus occurs when the pancreas doesn't produce enough insulin or because cells do not respond to the insulin that is produced. Insulin is required for the body to efficiently use sugars, fats and proteins. The commonest symptoms are increased thirst and urination. Although dogs with diabetes mellitus usually have a good appetite, there may be weight loss. Confusingly, some dogs become obese. In many cases cataracts (cloudy lenses in the eyes) may be the first sign that there is a problem. This disease may occur in conjunction with Cushing's syndrome, urinary tract infections, hypothyroidism, pancreatitis and cancer. The condition is usually diagnosed from a urine or blood test.

A natural raw food diet is excellent, but if you are changing the diet from a high-carbohydrate commercial diet the switch must be made under veterinary supervision.

Carbohydrates and acidity are the two core issues for diabetics. One of the reasons why commercial foods are not good for sufferers is that they usually contain urinary acidifiers. Urinary acidifiers can have the effect of complicating the acidosis most diabetics are already suffering from, and the carbohydrates in the diet just keep the problems coming.

If antibiotics are used as part of conventional treatment then prebiotics and probiotics are recommended. Other supplements that can help control the symptoms of diabetes mellitus include magnesium, fish oil, brewer's yeast, zinc and copper supplements and barley grass powder.

Exocrine pancreatic insufficiency

Exocrine pancreatic insufficiency (EPI) is the inability to properly digest food due to a lack of digestive enzymes made by the pancreas. It affects German Shepherds more than any other breed (about two-thirds of cases). EPI is caused by a progressive loss of the pancreatic cells that make digestive enzymes. It is often not diagnosed until well advanced. Symptoms include weight loss, poor hair coat, flatulence and a voracious appetite. Sufferers may also pass bulky, fatty stools.

In terms of treatment there is every reason to continue raw feeding since this is the easiest food for your dog to digest. The amount of fat consumed should be kept to a minimum: chicken and lean beef are both good. Avoid any food (including cooked vegetables such as carrots and peas) containing a high proportion of sugar as this forces the pancreas to work harder. Digestive enzymes and Tree Barks powder can help. It is important to make sure your dog has plenty of pure, clean water.

Hepatitis (liver disease)

The liver has five important functions, affecting circulation, excretion of waste products, metabolism, immunological defence and blood formation. There are two types of liver disease: primary and secondary. Primary is caused by a non- or sub-functioning liver; secondary is caused by some other condition, such as bacteria, viral parasites, poisons, toxins or tumours.

The most common symptoms associated with liver disease include loss of appetite, vomiting, abdominal pain, enlarged liver, jaundice, discoloured urine, oedema (swelling), weight loss, photosensitisation (skin disease related to sunlight), poor blood clotting, anaemia and a change in stools (either diarrhoea or constipation).

Once the cause has been treated, diet has an important role to play, especially in relation to the carbohydrate, fat, protein, vitamin and mineral content. Raw feeding is ideal as it is naturally low in protein and carbohydrate. Avoid all dairy and stick to a low-fat diet. Conventional treatment can lead to a compromised immune system, in which case food should be lightly cooked. If antibiotics have been used as part of the treatment then it is advisable to give your dog prebiotics and probiotics.

Impacted anal glands

Impacted anal glands are an extremely common problem for dogs. The glands are situated either side of the anus and discharge a foul-smelling liquid, which is used for marking territories. They are usually emptied by the passing of stools, or if the animal becomes frightened. If not emptied frequently they become impacted, which leads to infection and possibly an abscess being formed. Many vets feel that the primary cause of this problem is processed dog food.

If your dog licks under their tail a great deal, especially if it causes eczema, or if they drag their bottom along the ground, this could well be an anal gland problem. (However, the same symptoms could also be caused by worms.)

One of the benefits of a natural diet incorporating bone is that it creates small, firm stools, which empty the anal glands as the dog excretes.

Kidney disease (renal failure)

Kidney disease (or renal failure) is fairly common in dogs, especially those reaching their senior years. It is one of the few conditions where we do not recommend 100% raw feeding. Instead, you should take the same ingredients and par boil with lots of water and extra vegetables (especially green vegetables). The extra vegetables will reduce the level of animal protein. When cooking the meat, heat it until it changes colour and then leave it to finish cooking using its own heat.

A supplement called Udo's Beyond Greens will help throughput and to balance out the urea. Add it once the food has cooled and is ready to serve so as not to destroy the nutrients. Where high blood pressure is an issue, test to see whether the calcium, magnesium, potassium and sodium are all in the middle of the normal range. If below this level, add supplements. Cod liver oil, zinc and magnesium are very important dietary additions for patients with high blood pressure. *Solidago* (also called goldenrods) can also be of assistance. See below for more about kidney stones and purine problems.

Liver shunt

The medical term for liver shunt is portosystemic shunt (PSS). A 'shunt' is a blood vessel that bypasses the liver rather than passing through it. Dogs can be born with the condition or it may be acquired. Small dogs are affected more than larger dogs.

Diet has an important role to play in the treatment of liver shunt. Normally, the liver removes ammonia from the blood stream so when this isn't happening it is important to stop the body from producing ammonia in the first place. This can partly be achieved by a low-protein diet. Adding drugs like lactulose and ursodiol to the diet helps with this problem. Make sure the dog drinks plenty of water in order to avoid dehydration. A low-fat diet is best.

Homeopathic support for the liver can be very helpful and should be done under veterinary supervision. Low-potency organ support remedies such as chelidonium, *Carduus marianus*, *Taraxacum* and *Berberis* are recommended.

In some cases adding carbohydrate to the diet in the form of organic porridge oats soaked overnight in water can assist in reducing the protein percentage in the diet. Other suitable carbohydrate additions are polenta and brown rice.

Pancreatitis

The pancreas is a V-shaped organ located behind the stomach and the first section of the small intestine, known as the duodenum. It performs two main functions: it aids in the metabolism of sugar in the body through the production of insulin and is necessary for the digestion of food by producing pancreatic enzymes. Inflammation of the pancreas is called pancreatitis. The symptoms of the disease are a painful abdomen, abdominal distension, poor appetite, depression, dehydration, vomiting, diarrhoea and yellow, greasy stools. The dog may also look 'hunched up'.

There are various causes of pancreatitis, including certain medications, infections, metabolic disorders (high amounts of lipid or calcium in the blood), trauma and shock. Middle-aged dogs and dogs with diets high in fat and/or carbohydrates seem to be at most risk. It is thought that dogs who suffer from Cushing's disease (hyperadrenocorticism), hyperthyroidism and diabetes may also be at risk.

In terms of treatment there is every reason to continue raw feeding since this is the easiest food for your dog to digest. The amount of fat consumed should be kept to a minimum: chicken and lean beef are both good. Avoid any food (including vegetables such as carrots) containing a high proportion of sugar, as this forces the pancreas to work harder.

If the pancreas is totally non-functional or very sub-functional, medical supplements such as enzyme replacements may be necessary. This can be done with conventional enzyme replacements (such as Tryplase or Creon 2000) or herbal supplements (such as Tree Barks Powder from Dorwest Herbs).

Patients may also need antibiotics or steroids as part of a conventional treatment. One problem with conventional treatment is that patients can become immunocompromised as a result of the steroids, meaning that they will be more susceptible to infection even from the relatively normal bacteria in raw food. In such a case the food should be lightly cooked first.

KIDNEY STONES AND THE PURINE PROBLEM

If you have a Dalmatian, Beagle, Bulldog, Basset Hound, Cocker Spaniel, Bichon Frise, Miniature Schnauzer, Lhasa Apso, Miniature Poodle, Miniature Schnauzer, Yorkshire Terrier, Dachshund,

Newfoundland, Irish Terrier, Scottish Terrier or Irish Setter then you are probably only too aware that these breeds can have purine metabolism problems.

What are purines?

Purines are natural substances found in plant and animal cells that are vital to the chemical structure of genes. High levels of purine can be found in any food group (i.e. vegetables, fruit, meat and fish). Certain foods, such as kidneys, game, yeast, mackerel, herring, sardines and mussels have particularly high levels of purine. Others, such as chicken, beef, lamb and non-acidic fruit contain lower levels.

When cells die and get recycled in a dog's body the purines in their genetic material also get broken down. Once completely broken down they turn into uric acid, which is important to good health because it serves as an antioxidant that protects blood vessels.

However, sometimes uric acid levels in the blood and other parts of the body can become too high. This happens, for instance, when the kidney isn't functioning properly (as it is the kidney that helps keep blood levels of uric acid balanced) or where there is an excessive breakdown of cells. Although kidneys regulate the amount of purine (excreting what isn't required), it is worth remembering that the cause of the problem lies in the liver where purine metabolism takes place.

The purine problems in dogs...

The breeds already mentioned above metabolise purine in a unique way ending up with excess uric acid. This in turn leads to urate stones. Worse, if treated with allopurinol to block enzyme-producing urates, dogs can end up with xanthine stones instead of urate stones.

Urate stones are radiolucent and thus can easily be missed, especially when in the kidneys as X-rays pass right through them, leaving no shadow, unlike other stones. It takes air contrast X-rays to show them up. But this cannot be done in the kidney and the stone cannot be felt in the kidney, either. Even ultrasound can miss them but CT (computerised tomography) scanning can pick them up.

If you have a Dalmatian

Dalmatians are one breed that has been particularly prone to urinary stones and if you have a Dalmatian or are interested in why then this site will be of interest: www.thedca.org/stonecharts.html.

How can diet help?

A raw food diet without organ meat and with none of the high-purine vegetables (such as cauliflower, peas, spinach, mushrooms and legumes) is generally excellent as a diet for all breeds with a purine metabolism problem.

Commercial and homemade low-purine diets can make the condition worse rather than better.

In compromised dogs a high-fat diet can add to the problems by increasing urate formation, especially in the kidneys. So if you have a thin dog with a purine problem, consider increasing the frequency and size of meals rather than the fat level and check for hidden stones.

Bear in mind that plenty of pure water is also important. The word 'pure' must be emphasised as some additions to water for purification and sterilization purposes can change the urine pH or entire body chemistry, triggering crystal formation.

What else? 'Table foods' are out and so is anything with salt in it. With regard to diet, incidentally, this may require the addition of potassium citrates (for preventing calcium oxalate crystals) and sodium bicarbonate (for preventing cystine crystals). Always ensure that the diet does not have excessive amounts of vitamin C (ascorbic acid) added, as it acidifies urine, decreasing the risk of the most common forms of stones but increasing the risk of urates.

Finally, do remember to arrange regular urine checks to ensure that the pH stays alkaline and for the presence of either urate or xanthine crystals.

ORAL CONDITIONS

Gingivitis

Gingivitis is an infection of the gums and is often caused by the build-up of plaque on the teeth. Symptoms include bad breath, a sore mouth and consequent loss of appetite. Prevention is better than cure and chewing regularly on bones is to be recommended. There is a close connection between oral health and general health. There is every reason, therefore, to feed a raw diet.

Halitosis (bad breath)

The most common cause of bad breath is poor diet or poor oral health. The latter could be caused by bacteria, saliva and food particles forming plaque. A worse problem is periodontal disease, which can lead to gingivitis. Other possible causes include diabetes, kidney disease, gastrointestinal disease and infections in the area around the mouth. Respiratory diseases (for instance a sinus infection) and other oral diseases may be responsible. Finally, one should not rule out something that the dog is eating, such as household waste (or worse!). Obviously, the treatment will depend on the cause. Good dental hygiene can be achieved by chewing regularly on bones. There is a close connection between oral health and general health. There is every reason, therefore, to feed a raw diet.

SKIN CONDITIONS

Alopecia (fur loss)

There are many reasons why dogs may lose their coats. Some of the more common causes are allergies, bacterial, fungal or viral infections, mites and poor diet. Trauma to the skin from scratching, burns or wounds as well as stress and hormonal changes (as seen in Cushing's syndrome) may also be responsible. Dietary advice will depend on the underlying condition. A raw food diet will help, however, as it will rebalance the hormones and may even act as a natural hormone replacement (raw meat contains traces of hormones that dogs would be used to ingesting).

Itchy ears and skin problems caused by allergies

Itchiness, ear infections, fur loss and skin problems may be caused by a variety of issues, the most common of which is an allergy to food, grains, fleas, ticks, household chemicals, pollen or something else.

If the problem is a food allergy it could well be the result of eating grain or grain-fed meat (intensively reared beef and chicken are often responsible).

Traditionally, vets have treated ear and skin problems of this type with a course of antibiotics and steroids, desensitising injections and creams such as cyclosporine A.

Before treatment can be started, it is important to identify the cause of the allergy. In the case of any food allergy the switch to a natural diet may solve the problem, especially as it will help to support the immune system. If the patient has taken antibiotics, a course of prebiotics and probiotics is recommended. One of the ways in which the body responds to a skin-related allergy is to release histamine and other chemicals. Omega 3 can, sometimes, reduce the effects of histamine. Note that other fatty acids, such as omega 6, can actually worsen some allergies.

Itchy skin

Apart from allergies (see above), there are many different reasons why dogs suffer from itchy skin, including mites, demodex and mange. Until the cause is known, it is difficult to recommend a treatment, but the following tips may help:

- Various oils reduce inflammation, including cod liver oil, evening primrose oil and starflower oil.
- Consider adding vitamin C to the diet. At least 1000mg daily and even more if the dog can absorb it without diarrhoea.
- If you are taking a dog off medication, use a broad-spectrum multivitamin that includes magnesium as this will dampen down the side effects.
- If the dog has been given antibiotics, a course of prebiotics and probiotics is recommended.

Homeopathic remedies can be very helpful alongside conventional medicine in these cases.

Paw chewing

If your dog is chewing its paws, the first step is to check that there are no foreign bodies, such as eggshell splinters, thorns or glass, present and that he or she hasn't sustained a cut. If the dog is on processed food, the cause may be dietary since grain can produce this symptom. A raw food diet is to be recommended. If the cause is boredom then giving the dog a bone may solve the problem. If persistent check the dog's urine for a kidney problem. It may also be worth checking for a thyroid problem.

OTHER CONDITIONS

Arthritis

Depending upon who you talk to, the terms 'arthritis', 'osteoarthritis' and 'degenerative joint disease' may or may not be used to describe the same thing.

Degenerative joint disease is characterised by the loss of the smooth cartilage that covers and protects the ends of the bones in a movable joint. The cartilage has no nerves so when it touches the cartilage of another bone there is no pain. When the cartilage wears away, the bone is exposed and, since bones do have nerves, pain and inflammation are caused by the two ends in a joint touching each other. This is the sign that arthritis is present and will probably be progressive. In degenerative joint disease, small bony projections known as osteophytes form on the bone that is closest to the joint.

Degenerative joint disease can occur as a result of wear and tear on an otherwise normal joint and occurs as the dog ages. Osteoarthritis may also occur as a result of hip dysplasia or elbow dysplasia.

A raw food diet helps arthritis because it is low in carbohydrates. High-carbohydrate diets create an excessively acid bloodstream, decreasing uric acid solubility, which in turn leads to joint pain. Bones are an important part of the diet and should include joint bones for their cartilage content (high in chondroitin sulphate) and the marrow of bones including chicken (chicken bones have lots of glucosamine). Turkey is also a good source and, importantly, much lower in salt than most commercial supplements. Such a diet often does away with the need for such supplements as glucosamine and chondroitin, or lowers the required dose.

Supplements that help arthritic pets include cod liver, evening primrose and star flower oil, vitamin C, green-lipped mussel, turmeric, ginger and boswellia (between 1/16th and 1/8th of a teaspoon only), black treacle (also known as blackstrap molasses), the herbs devil's and cat's claw.

Cancers and tumours

One of the ways in which many cancers and tumours can be starved is to reduce the carbohydrates in the diet to 20% or under. (Bear in mind that most commercial dog foods contain 60% or more carbohydrates.) The purity of the food – ideally it should be organic – and the water is crucial. The vegetables should be as fresh as possible as after a few days vegetables start to lose their nutritional value. Of the many different supplements that can help cancer patients, vitamin C is perhaps the most important: 1000mg a day (or more) is recommended. Please contact Honey's Real Dog Food if you would like more specific advice.

Discospondylitis

Discospondylitis (diskospondylitis or vertebral osteomyelitis) is a bacterial or fungal infection of the vertebrae and the intervertebral discs. The resulting inflammation and swelling along with the bone deformities put pressure on the spinal cord, which runs through the vertebrae. Feed the dog a natural diet. Supplements to consider include vitamin C and zinc. Give the dog a natural probiotic.

Elbow dysplasia

Elbow dysplasia is more common in fast-growing larger-breed dogs while they are still puppies. Dogs with elbow dysplasia usually have a limp and may hold the leg out from the body when walking. Some will avoid putting any weight on the leg at all. As many sufferers mature, the symptoms may become less severe. Medication may be needed to reduce pain. Some dogs may need surgery and others will have an altered elbow joint with arthritis from a young age. Feed a raw food diet with plenty of bone such as chicken wings, chicken thighs, drumsticks, pork ribs and marrow bones. Supplement with oil (fish, evening primrose or hemp oil) and vitamin C. Do not allow the dog to over-exercise.

Epilepsy

Epilepsy is a disorder of recurring seizures. Epileptic fits are the result of a sort of short-circuiting of the nerves in the brain, so that many nerves are stimulated at once. This can result in quite violent body spasms. Not all dogs that have seizures are epileptic; fits can happen for a number of reasons. For example, older dogs may have an underlying heart, kidney or liver condition, or there may be a tumour on the brain. This last possibility is, thankfully, not all that common. Traumatic injuries to the head can lead to fits in any age dog, as can infections, such as viral or bacterial ones. Occasionally, poisons, such as slug pellets (metaldehyde), will cause a dog to fit. In any of the above cases it is important to treat the underlying problem, if possible, and so eliminate or control the fits that way.

Diet has an important role to play in the treatment of epilepsy. Meats low in glutamate, such as lamb, are best. Avoid meat from animals that have been fed a grain diet. Avoid rabbit, turkey and oily fish, as all are high in glutamate. Epilepsy is definitely on the rise and the combination of wheat and soy in pet foods may well be responsible. Eggs (again low in glutamate) are a good source of nutrition. In addition to the above, one should try to ensure the diet is free of chemicals (preservatives, taste enhancers, palatability factors, chemical antioxidants and so forth), making organic ingredients ideal. Processed foods are particularly bad for epileptic dogs as they are high in grain and incorporate rancid fats.

Hip dysplasia

Hip dysplasia is associated with abnormal joint structure and a laxity in the muscles, connective tissue and ligaments that normally support the joint. As the laxity develops, the head of the femur and socket joint separate. This is known as subluxation. Most dogs are born with normal hips; however, owing to their genetic makeup and possibly other factors, the soft tissues surrounding the joint develop abnormally, causing subluxation that leads to altered gait and/or lameness. One or both hips may be affected. Feed a raw food diet with plenty of bone such as chicken wings, chicken thighs, drumsticks, pork ribs and marrow bones. Supplement with oil (fish, evening primrose or hemp oil) and vitamin C. Do not allow the dog to over-exercise.

Lafora

Lafora disease (sometimes called Lafora progressive myoclonic epilepsy) is an inherited form of epilepsy that can occur spontaneously in any breed of dog, but it particularly affects the Miniature Wire-haired Dachshund, Basset Hound and Beagle. There is a website (www.laforadogs.org) which is asking for testing to be done for the breeds at risk so that dogs who are carriers are no longer used for breeding. The same dietary advice as for epilepsy (see above) is recommended.

Luxating patella

Luxating patella only occurs in certain breeds, particularly small dogs with short legs, and describes a process whereby one leg bone jumps out of its socket. When it occurs, the leg locks up with the foot held off the ground. It cannot return to its normal position until the quadriceps muscle relaxes and increases in length. Typically, a small dog will be running and then in mid-stride yelp, hold up the back leg and then continue as if nothing is wrong. After a time, the leg drops back down and is used normally. The lameness is very intermittent and does not seem to worry the dog. A raw food diet is excellent. Ensure plenty of bone. Keep the dog from becoming overweight as this will worsen the symptoms.

Osteochondritis dissecans

Osteochondritis dissecans, or OCD (not obsessive–compulsive disorder!), is a disease of the cartilage which may affect the shoulder, elbow, knee or hock. Some dogs will barely have a limp, while others may not want to put any weight on the affected leg. Lameness can worsen after exercise and improves after resting.

It is caused by many factors, including genetics, trauma, rapid growth and poor nutrition. The conventional treatment is strict rest, an NSAID (non-steroidal anti-inflammatory drug) such as carprofen or surgery to remove the damaged cartilage.

It is important that the dog does not become overweight. Feed a raw food diet. Ensure plenty of bone. Supplements which may help include oil (fish, evening primrose, starflower and/or hemp) and vitamin C.

Spondylosis

Spondylosis is a non-infectious fusion or degeneration of the vertebrae. The dog is stiff after getting up, appears to be limping (especially after exercise) or begins snapping or licking the lower back. Occasionally, a bony spur or fusing of the vertebrae will cause loss of bladder control and the dog will become incontinent. Feed the dog a natural diet. Supplements to consider include tumeric, ginger, boswellic acids, cat's claw, devil's claw, green-lipped mussel, cod liver oil and glucosamine. It is important that the dog isn't allowed to jump up.

Von Willebrand disease

Von Willebrand disease is a common inherited bleeding disorder similar to haemophilia in humans. Because of the risk of bleeding not being stopped, these dogs need to be looked after very carefully. As even a tiny scratch can cause a problem, patients should not be given any bones. To compensate for potential blood loss a diet high in iron (such as liver) is recommended perhaps two or three times a week. To compensate for the lack of bones a human-grade bone meal should be added to the food so that the patient receives around 700mg of calcium every day. Fish oil is an anti-inflammatory and will protect the kidneys, so one or two teaspoons (depending on the size of the dog) every day is recommended. (If you can't obtain fish oil then cod liver oil is an alternative, although not quite as effective.) Aloe vera with cranberry juice can also help to protect the kidneys; give 20–60ml (depending on size of dog) three times a week.

Some sufferers of von Willebrand disease haemorrhage frequently, especially internally, and can develop uremia. Additionally, if the problem is autoimmune, where the body attacks its own clotting factors, then the kidneys operate even less effectively. Diet has an important role to play here, too. If the dog is in the uremic stage then raw chicken is recommended. The dog should be given plenty of fluids to keep the kidneys flushed through.

A WORD ABOUT STEROIDS

Steroids can produce unpleasant side effects (including lethargy, excessive hunger and excessive thirst) and may even cause diabetic-type syndrome. Before putting your dog on a course of steroids, consider consulting a holistic vet to see what other options are available.

13.
ANSWERING THE ARGUMENTS AGAINST NATURAL FEEDING

THIRTEEN

Raw feeding is an emotive subject and you may be surprised at how many people try to dissuade you from switching your dog to a natural diet.

The arguments against raw feeding can be very convincing if you don't know the real facts, especially as they are often backed up by vets and other experts.

Myth one: Dogs aren't wolves

One of the main reasons why natural feeding makes such sense is that dogs and wolves are the same species, the only difference being that dogs have been domesticated.

It is sometimes suggested that because dogs have been domesticated their physiology and digestive systems have evolved and no longer resemble those of the wolf. Therefore, the argument goes, the idea that they should eat the same diet as wolves (or wild dogs) is wrong.

This line of reasoning falls apart both in the bedroom and on the dissecting table! Wolves and dogs can interbreed. The digestive system of a Chihuahua and the digestive system of a wolf are identical in everything but scale. Yes, dogs may have been eating a certain amount of cooked food for the last 8,000–20,000 years but (a) it has only been a percentage of their diet, (b) it is has only been a percentage of domesticated dogs and (c) it hasn't been long enough for them to change the way their bodies digest and absorb nutrients.

The idea (sometimes suggested) that dogs have adapted to processed food since it was invented in 1860 is laughable. It is possible for species to partially adapt to a new diet but palaeontologists believe that it takes at least 100,000 years and probably a great deal longer.

Myth two: Raw food is home to (dangerous) salmonella

You can pretty much ignore anything anyone says to you about the dangers of salmonella poisoning in relation to raw feeding.

Salmonella poses a very, very low risk to humans and an even lower risk to dogs. It is present in 80% to 85% of all raw chicken and yet the number of people who actually suffer from salmonella poisoning is tiny. It is even rarer for a dog to suffer from it and it is interesting to note that when tests were done and dogs were fed infected meat only one-third had any evidence at all of salmonella in their faeces. In other words, the canine stomach acids (which are strong enough to burn your fingers) killed the vast majority of it off.

So, what is salmonella? Salmonella is a bacterium that can cause some unpleasant reactions in our gastrointestinal system, like vomiting and diarrhoea, and often fever. The attack may last about a week. There was some interesting research done in the US which showed that people have a risk of about 0.25% per year of getting infected with salmonella, and 0.05 ppm (ppm = 'parts per million') of dying of a salmonella infection. To put this in perspective, this compares to a yearly risk of 108 ppm for a man (33 ppm for a woman) getting murdered, about 100 ppm for getting killed in a car accident and 11 ppm for a person less than 91 years old to die of influenza or pneumonia.

What chance is there of a human catching it from a dog? Dogs do not carry salmonella in their saliva or on their skin, not even after eating 100% salmonella-infected raw food. But, when they do eat salmonella-infected food, about one-third of them will show a moderate concentration of salmonella in their faeces – yet no clinical signs of being sick. The only way a human can catch salmonella from a dog is by, to put it bluntly, eating its you-know-what!

Incidentally, dogs eating a processed food diet are just as likely to have salmonella in their system, as it is easy to pick up in parks and elsewhere.

Human beings have been made paranoid about bacteria. In fact, there are more bacteria on a shopping trolley handle than on a piece of raw chicken.

Myth three: Raw food contains dangerous parasites

In the wild, dogs will usually go for the easiest prey, often animals that are frail and sick. They also eat meat that is rotten, meat that has been buried for weeks and then dug up and, of course, meat that contains parasites. In all these instances they suffer no, or very few, ill effects.

Nevertheless, it is sometimes argued that raw feeding is dangerous to canine and human health because the meat may contain parasites.

This is incorrect for two reasons. First, the food-borne parasites to which dogs are vulnerable do not pose any risk to humans. Second, a dog's stomach acids are so strong that they destroy almost all known food-borne parasites likely to be of harm to them.

If you are still worried about parasites, freeze the food first for at least 24 hours. This will deal with all but a very few, very rare parasites that are never found in food suitable for human consumption.

Myth four: Raw fed dogs are at risk from neospora

Neospora is a very interesting issue, especially as it was only discovered relatively recently. There have been lots of studies on its effect in cattle but there is almost no research in relation to dogs. Neospora is a parasite and, so far, it seems to be very prevalent in beef herds: up to 80% of them are infected.

Can it be transmitted from cattle to dogs via meat? If it can, what effect does it have on the dog? Finally, is there any risk to humans? There have been so few cases reported in dogs that there is almost nothing to go on. The dogs that seem most at risk are puppies and dogs with compromised immune systems. It seems to follow the same model as toxoplasmosis and coccidiosis. But there are no properly documented cases of it affecting raw fed dogs. Amongst pro-raw feeding vets, the basic feeling is that if it were a serious risk we would be hearing a lot more about it.

There is no need to worry about this risk, especially as neospora has probably been present in dogs and cattle for hundreds of thousands of years.

Myth five: Raw fed dogs are at risk of renal failure

It has been suggested that feeding a dog bones puts them at risk of renal failure, owing to the high amount of calcium/phosphorous to be found in a natural diet.

Calcium is vital to your dog's health and is the most common mineral in the body. The majority of it (99%) is in the bones, with the rest distributed between other tissues and blood. Calcium has an indispensable role in major bodily functions. It is required for the transmission of nerve impulses. It is required for muscle contraction. It is a vital component in the blood-clotting mechanism. It is the structural component of bones and, hence, is of vital importance in growing animals.

Phosphorous is the other dietary mineral required in a relatively high amount in the diet. About 80% of phosphorus in the body is found in bones and teeth, principally as apatite salts and as calcium phosphate. It is located in every cell of the body. Phosphorus is also intimately involved in the acid base buffer system of blood and other bodily fluids, as a component of cell walls and cell contents as phospholipids, phospho-proteins and nucleic acids. Chronic signs of deficiency include rickets in young animals and osteomalacia in adults, poor growth and lactation performance, and unsatisfactory fertility. Phosphorous is required at levels slightly less than calcium. Meat or organ meats are relatively high in phosphorous but relatively low in calcium.

It is completely wrong to say that raw feeding, eating bones and meat, causes renal failure! To begin with in a well-balanced raw food diet they will be in the correct proportions. Then there is the fact that raw food has lower levels of phosphorous than most canned or dried food. Plus the idea that a high-protein diet increases the chance of renal failure has been pretty much blown out of the water as rubbish.

Myth six: Raw fed dogs are at risk of choking on bones

Bones, it is suggested, can cause dogs to choke or may rupture the stomach or intestine. In fact, dogs are more than capable of digesting raw, uncooked bones. This is thanks to their strong stomach acids. They are much more likely to choke on dried, processed food, which usually has a water content of between 5% and 10%, far below the 70% water content of a natural diet.

Myth seven: Raw food is covered in bacteria

Yes, it is! But dogs are surprisingly well equipped to deal with bacteria. Their saliva contains lysozyme, an enzyme that destroys harmful bacteria. Their short digestive tract is designed to push through food and bacteria quickly without giving bacteria time to colonise. The extremely acidic environment in the gut is also a good bacteria colonisation deterrent.

Incidentally, processed dog food is as much of a risk in terms of bacteria as this quote proves: 'Pet foods, commercial or homemade, provide an ideal environment for bacterial proliferation' (LeJuene, J. T. and D. D. Hancock. 2001. Public health concerns associated with feeding raw meat diets to dogs. *Journal of the American Veterinary Medical Association* 219(9): 1224.). The starches, rancid fats and sugars in kibbled foods provide much better food sources for bacteria than the proteins in raw meat do.

14.
A CHAPTER ABOUT SOMETHING NO ONE LIKES TO MENTION

FOURTEEN

There's no point in beating about the bush: this chapter is about your dog's poo. Why? Because it is an important indicator of your dog's health.

Before we tackle the nitty-gritty (as it were) of this subject, some good news.

Dogs on a raw food diet produce much less excrement, and what little there is of it biodegrades quickly and doesn't smell.

Normal? What's normal?

A normal stool should be soft, yet firm. Its colour will be determined by the dog's diet: anything from a mid-brown to nearly black is usual. The more meat in the diet, the softer and darker it tends to be.

If you want to firm your dog's stools up, the simplest way is to add bone.

It is normal to find a greyish bag of slime around your dog's stool from time to time. This is the old mucous membrane, which the intestine sheds every few months.

It is also normal to see the remains of vegetables in the stool. This is vegetable matter the dog hasn't digested and it helps to stimulate the mechanical function of the intestine.

A reason to be firm

It is important that your dog passes relatively firm (even quite hard) stools on a regular basis. Why? In the area under the tail, dogs have two anal glands. These excrete a particular smell when dogs move their bowels, thus allowing them to mark territory and so identify other dogs.

Dog faeces are normally firm, and the anal glands usually empty when the dog defecates, lubricating the anal opening in the process. When the dog's stools are soft, they may not exert enough pressure on the glands, which then may fail to empty. This may cause discomfort as the full anal gland pushes on the anus. If you see a dog pulling its bottom along the floor it could well be because its anal glands are causing it a problem.

Stool guide

- **Very dark or black**
  This is caused by a high percentage of meat in the diet, especially liver and other offal.

- **Greyish**
  Usually the result of eating grain and/or processed food.

- **Light-coloured stool**
  Especially if greyish. May be caused by a liver or pancreatic problem, so worth consulting your vet.

- **Greasy stool**
  When dogs have a pancreatic problem, they are unable to digest fat efficiently. A greasy, sour-smelling stool may be an indication of an underlying pancreatic issue. Discuss with your vet.

- **Foamy stool**
  Could be an infection in the intestine or colon as a result of undigested fat. Again, you should probably discuss with your vet.

- **Very hard stool**
  If your dog is on a processed food diet then the cause is probably one of the ingredients included to keep the stools firm: it is not unknown for dog food companies to use sawdust for this purpose! If your dog is on a raw food diet, a hard stool is usually the result of a healthy meal of bone.

- **Blood in the stool**
  This may be caused by anything from a parasite (such as a worm) to a stool that is too firm. You should keep a sample (sorry!) to show to your vet. Bear in mind that the blood may not be red. If it is not fresh, it may appear almost black.

Soft and runny stools

A soft, runny or watery stool is not necessarily anything to worry about unless it lasts for several days or is combined with other symptoms (such as blood in the stool or vomiting). It is normal for stools to be soft, runny or watery when a dog changes diet or eats something that it doesn't want to digest.

Why raw food produces so much less waste

Mogens Eliasen, a raw feeding expert, has published information about the volume of stools compared to the volume of food being eaten. Meat, offal and animal fat are almost completely digested. The amount of excrement produced will represent between 2% and 7% of the food being eaten. Fruit and vegetables produce around 30% to 60% waste. Kibble, on the other hand, produces 60% to 80% waste. This is because dogs are able to take a great deal of nutrition from meat, organs and animal fat but not from processed food.

When to be worried about diarrhoea

If your dog has diarrhoea for more than three days, or if it has diarrhoea one day, normal stools for a few days, and then diarrhoea again until it ends up mostly having diarrhoea, then the problem may be worms.

If your dog has diarrhoea together with another symptom, such as blood in the stool, vomiting, fever or a change in behaviour, then you should consult your vet.

NO ONE LIKES TO MENTION…

Good news for your garden

Naturally fed dogs produce less excrement and what they produce breaks down quickly. As it has no harmful chemicals in it, it won't damage your lawn. If you feed your dog raw food there will be fewer chemicals in its urine, too. This will mean that the urine should not damage your grass or turn it yellow.

15.
NATURAL FEEDING
FOR CATS

FIFTEEN

Your cat will flourish on a biologically appropriate diet. What evidence do I have of this? In the next chapter I review Pottenger's Cats, a book that describes a ten-year experiment involving 900 cats, which led to the discovery that raw fed cats live substantially longer, healthier lives.

Most cats love raw food from the moment you switch, and those that don't generally come to love it within a week or two.

What should cats be eating?

What is a biologically appropriate diet for cats? Cats are obligate carnivores. In other words, they can't survive on vegetables and fruit. In the wild, cats eat prey (mice, birds, voles, insects &c.) and in a more domestic setting this needs to be replicated with raw meat and raw bone. Almost everything I have written in this book about feeding dogs a natural diet applies to cats, with the exceptions outlined below.

About kibble fed cats

If you feed a cat a high carbohydrate diet – particularly if it consists of a dry kibble – then he or she may become addicted to the blood glucose 'high' that the food is providing. Such cats are generally hungry most of the time and will keep asking for more and more food. Almost all processed cat food is heavily flavoured with 'palatability enhancers', and this is another reason why some cats are so keen on it. Incidentally, some vets feel that kibble is the cause of dehydration in cats.

Your cat's new diet

Your cat's diet should largely consist of raw meat and raw bone.

As cats love variety, test lots of different ingredients: poultry, red meat and fish (although not too much herring as it can contain thiaminase which destroys vitamin B1). The most natural ingredients are smaller prey: rabbit, wild game, chicken and duck.

Cats need raw bones and it is important that they chew. Favourites include chicken necks, wings and drumsticks.

Offal meat is excellent but shouldn't account for more than 5% to 10% of the diet.

Some vegetable matter is good for cats – you can feed between 5% and 10% of the diet.

Unless you are feeding your cat fish on a regular basis I would recommend adding fish oil (500mg) every day. If your cat is allergic to fish oil, coconut oil or coconut milk are both excellent sources of omega-3 fatty acid.

A healthy adult cat will eat 5% to 10% of its bodyweight every day.

Making the switch

1. The first and most important thing is to stop making food available all the time. Don't leave a bowl of food on the floor. Create specific mealtimes – between two and five a day to begin with, reducing to one or two. This will ensure that your cat is actually hungry when you serve the raw food. Note, if the cat doesn't eat the food within a few minutes put it back in the fridge. If it looks a little grey after being in the fridge mix it up with a spoon.

2. Try gently warming the food (some cats don't like it cold). This can be done by mixing a couple of teaspoons of boiling water into it or standing bowl in boiling water. Never be tempted to put it in the microwave.

3. Try mixing it with the existing food. Use a very little raw food to begin with and gradually (very gradually) alter the proportions. This 'weaning' on to raw food can take as long as 10 weeks. There is no hurry, go with the pace of your cat.

4. Other things you could add to encourage eating include tinned or fresh fish, prawns, or a little scrambled egg.

5. Cats will drink less water once they are on a raw food diet because there's more water in the actual food.

6. If a cat has soft stools or diarrhoea then add a pinch or two of slippery elm (this is excellent for most digestive disorders and can be found in Tree Barks Powder from Dorwest.com), brewer's yeast or psyllium husk to the food.

'I had been told,' said Bill Dana, 'that the training procedure with cats was difficult. It's not. Mine had me trained in two days.' Cats, perhaps more than any other species on earth, seem determined to have their own way. This is especially true when it comes to food. Take the switching process slowly and steadily.

Pregnant mums and kittens

Pregnant and feeding mums will need extra food.

When the time comes to wean the kittens onto solid food start with ground raw meat and ground raw bone. A small amount of soft cheese or yoghurt is good. As soon as possible introduce them to hard bones. A raw chicken wing is an excellent starting point.

A newly weaned kitten will eat between one and two teaspoons of food four times a day. From 12 to 16 weeks cut back to three times daily but slightly increase the volume of food. Thereafter reduce to once or twice a day by six months.

Kittens need between 5% and 10% of their bodyweight in food every day. If they are growing quickly feed them closer to 10%.

A word about taurine

One of the ways in which processed food manufacturers have tried to rubbish raw feeding for cats is to suggest that a natural (biologically appropriate) diet doesn't contain enough taurine. No scientist has been able to show precisely how much taurine cats ought to eat. However, high levels of taurine exist in all the meats I am suggesting you serve your cat. This is how they would obtain it in the wild. The taurine issue is a red herring (which also contains high levels of the stuff).

We are happy to help

Although Honey's is, essentially, a dog food company we do have lots of experience raw feeding cats. If you have any cat diet or cat health questions, please do get in touch. Incidentally, our vegetable-free recipes are ideal for cats.

16.
OTHER SOURCES OF
INFORMATION

HELPING DOGS AND CATS TO GET THE FOOD THAT NATURE INTENDED THEM TO EAT

Looking for a vet or trainer who recommends raw feeding? Want more information on the whole subject? Please do get in touch with us at Honey's. You can consult our own vet and veterinary nurses and/or we may be able to recommend someone who lives near you. Please remember, we are happy to provide advice and support without cost or obligation. We will be delighted to help even if you never plan to become a customer.

SIXTEEN

Further reading

'Always read something', suggested P. J. O'Rourke, 'that will make you look good if you die in the middle of it.' I am not quite sure how you would look if you keeled over with a book about canine diet in your hands. Earnest, I suppose. At any rate, you wouldn't (and this may surprise you) die of boredom. Because, like many specialist topics, once you get into it, canine diet is fascinating. In fact, my chief complaint is that although there are a number of really good books on the subject more have not been written. 'Outside of a dog,' advised Groucho Marx, 'a book is man's best friend. Inside of a dog it's too dark to read.' Quite where that leaves books about dogs' insides I am not entirely sure, but here are details of my favourites.

Real Food for Dogs and Cats
Dr Clare Middle
This book isn't long but it is well written and provides a comprehensive and easy-to-understand guide to raw feeding. The first three chapters are aimed at dog owners, and the second three chapters at cat owners. Middle is good at explaining quite complicated topics and manages to make them interesting, too. There are lots of practical tips and straightforward recipes. Contains details of relevant raw feeding research.

Natural Nutrition for Dogs and Cats
Kathy Schultze
Another short and comprehensive book on raw feeding with lots of tips and advice. Schultze takes quite a strong line on certain ingredients (such as dairy and honey), which more relaxed raw

feeders may not feel so strongly about. There is a great deal of good information in this book and it is not expensive.

Give Your Dog a Bone
Dr Ian Billinghurst
Give Your Dog a Bone by Dr Ian Billinghurst, an Australian vet, was the first popular book to promote the idea of feeding dogs raw food and meaty bones. Indeed, its author is generally credited with promoting the term BARF, which stands for 'Biologically Appropriate Raw Food'. However, there is no mention of BARF in this first book, which starts by exploding some of the modern dog food myths (basically, that processed food is good for dogs) and goes on to explain why so many common canine health issues are actually caused by processed food. Having set the scene, he then discusses the ideal canine diet and provides all the information you need to prepare it yourself. There are separate chapters on the key ingredients and on feeding puppies and older dogs. This book really brought raw feeding to a wider audience and is as relevant today as it was when it was first published.

The BARF Diet
Dr Ian Billinghurst
Dr Billinghurst's second book on raw feeding repeats much of the same material as his first book (see above) but includes lots of extra information, too. Billinghurst's style can be a little repetitive, but that shouldn't put you off! He knows his stuff and was really the first vet to go public with the problems of processed food.

Grow Your Pups with Bones
Dr Ian Billinghurst
This book is, as its title implies, aimed at breeders. It contains lots of useful information on feeding pregnant mums, new mums and puppies. The author explains how diet can improve fertility and there is a fascinating section on skeletal disease and its connection with diet. In particular, Billinghurst suggests that many of the genetic problems blamed on overbreeding may well be the result of feeding dogs a processed food diet for several decades.

Raw Meaty Bones: Promote Health

Tom Lonsdale

Tom Lonsdale, a British-born vet, has been fighting a long and bloody battle with the various veterinary professional bodies over canine and feline diet. In particular, he has accused the majority of vets and the organisations that represent them of being 'bought' by the pet food industry. In *Raw Meaty Bones*, published in 2001, he has gathered an impressive body of research to prove his main point, that a raw food diet involving meaty bones is by far the best thing that dogs (and cats) can eat. He highlights all the problems with processed food and offers hard scientific evidence that companion animals thrive on raw food. The book contains some dietary advice but mostly it is concerned with the damage being done to dogs and cats by the processed pet food industry. The chapters relating to periodontal disease are eye-openers. If you are interested in the theory more than the practice (and if you would like to learn exactly why some people think the pet food industry is heading for a massive scandal) then this is the book to buy.

Dogs, Diet and Disease

Caroline Levin

This book is invaluable for a number of reasons. First of all, it explains how canine metabolism and endocrine functions work in a normal dog. In other words, the author provides a relatively plain-English guide to your dog's innards. Second, she offers a really good section on diet, reviewing the options, including commercially produced food, home-prepared food and raw food. Third, she has done her homework. The book contains details of all the relevant studies of the effects of processed dog food compared to raw dog food. Incidentally, if your dog suffers from any sort of disease (diabetes, pancreatitis, Cushing's &c.) then this book is a must as it contains lots of advice.

Foods Pets Die For: Shocking Facts about Pet Foods

Ann N. Martin

For seven years Canadian author Ann Martin researched the American pet food industry and *Food Pets Die For: Shocking Facts about Pet Foods* is the result. It is not short of the 'shocking facts' mentioned in the title, either. Did you know, for instance, that road kill, dead pets and zoo animals end up in pet food? Or that they don't hesitate to use beaks, feathers and even more disgusting ingredients in their products? Martin is great on why processed food is so bad, but not as sound on the best alternative. Indeed, if you search for her book on Amazon and read the reviews you will see that some readers have been quite severe in their criticism. Nevertheless, she did a wonderful job exposing the appalling behaviour of giant pet food manufacturers and the book is worth reading for this alone.

Raw Food for Dogs: The Ultimate Reference for Dog Owners!
Mogens Eliasen
Eliasen is a somewhat eccentric individual. He was formerly in the Danish army, where he ran their canine division, although he also seems to have been part of their intelligence operations, too. He is an entrepreneur with several successful small- to medium-size businesses to his name and has written extensively on international tax planning. For all that, he is extremely sound when it comes to raw feeding and clearly spent years researching the subject. His highly readable books are available for download from the Internet, including my favourite: *Raw Food for Dogs*. Visit www.mogenseliasen.com for more information.

Not Fit for a Dog! The Truth about Manufactured Dog and Cat Food
Michael Fox, Elizabeth Hodgkins and Marion Smart
The title says it all. Another excellent book on the dangers of modern pet food. It explodes the myths propounded by pet food companies that human food is bad for pets, and that natural food diets are unsafe. Written by three vets, it sets out the arguments for raw food but then, weirdly, goes on to recommend cooking the recommended ingredients. Still, packed with interesting information and research.

Pottenger's Cats: A Study in Nutrition
Frances Pottenger
This is a thrilling read for anyone interested in the scientific rationale for raw food. Dr Pottenger discovered, quite by accident, that cats' health degenerated unless they were fed raw food. In

his 10-year study of 900 cats, he found the optimal diet for his cats was two-thirds raw meat and one-third raw milk, plus a little cod liver oil. If either the meat or the milk were cooked, the cats degenerated. And if both were cooked, the degeneration was much worse, and the cats could no longer reproduce by the third generation. Conclusive proof that raw feeding produces healthier, longer-living pets.

Pet Food Politics: The Chihuahua in the Coal Mine
Marion Nestle
This book tells the story of the largest consumer product recall in history involving, as you will have gathered, pet food. It reads a bit like a detective story, and, although the main theme is the greed of pet food manufacturers, Nestle reveals a great deal about how processed food is made and, of course, what is wrong with it. A chilling but gripping yarn.

From the USA

There are three books only available in the USA that I can also strongly recommend. They can be expensive to buy in the UK, but no raw food library would be complete without them. The first is *Dr. Becker's Real Food for Healthy Dogs & Cats* by Beth Taylor and Karen Shaw Becker, which contains a brilliant explanation as to why dogs should be eating a natural diet and lots of recipes. The second is *Raw & Natural Nutrition for Dogs* by Lew Olson, which I particularly like for its plain-English approach to quite complicated subjects (well, complicated if one only just scraped through biology at school). Finally, Steve Brown's *Unlocking the Canine Ancestral Diet* contains fascinating original research into what dogs would eat in the wild and how best to replicate it using 'domestic' ingredients.

Top raw food websites

Honey's Real Dog Food

www.honeysrealdogfood.com

Articles by Tom Lonsdale

www.rawmeatybones.com

Articles by Dr. Karen Becker

http:healthypets.mercola.com

Making raw feeding easy

www.rawlearning.com

A raw feeder's experience and advice

www.rawfed.com

Another raw feeder's experience and more advice

www.rawfeddogs.net

Primal Pooch (blog)

www.primalpooch.com

The Natural Dog

www.rawfddogs.org

Top 50 frequently asked raw food questions

www.njboxers.com/faqs.htm

UK Raw Meaty Bones

www.ukrmb.co.uk

17.
HONEY'S REAL DOG FOOD

SEVENTEEN

As I explained in Chapter 1, I have written this book because although there are some excellent reference works on raw feeding I couldn't find a short, plain-English, practical guide to the subject.

It is based on my own experience as the founder of an artisan dog food business, Honey's Real Dog Food, which is responsible for raw feeding over 4,000 dogs a month.

My friend Vicky and I launched Honey's (it was originally called Darling's, but we had to change the name for complicated legal reasons) because we believe passionately that all dogs should be fed a natural diet.

For this reason we are happy to provide unlimited advice and support to anyone who wants to make the switch, even if they never plan to become a customer. So, if you have any questions not answered in these pages please contact us.

Meanwhile, this final chapter explains what we do at Honey's.

We'll feed your dog our delicious raw food FREE for a week!

Before I say another word, I just want to mention our new customer offer. If you are interested in trying our food out for a month we will give you the first week free of charge. Alternatively, new customers can try a smaller quantity of our food with a Half Price Hamper.

We make feeding a natural diet incredibly easy

At Honey's we make it incredibly easy to feed your dog a natural diet. Our raw, fresh dog food is produced using lean, minced meat (choose from a variety of seasonal recipes including free-range chicken, pork, beef and lamb as well as wild rabbit and other game) and grated vegetables. What about the all-important bone element – so crucial to your dog's health? We grind the bone (so that it can barely be seen) and mix it in. We also supply individual bones in convenient sizes as well as chicken wings, handmade biscuits and treats. I will come back to the subject in a moment, but I want to stress that we are deeply concerned about animal welfare and the environment. To the best of my knowledge, for instance, we are the only dog food producer in the UK that doesn't use any intensively reared meat. Incidentally, if you want to go the DIY route we can also help. See below.

A very personal approach

One of the first things you'll notice if you decide to feed your dog Honey's is that we take a very personal approach. It isn't just that we want to know your dog's name; we also want to know his or her vital statistics, medical history, lifestyle, preferences and personality. We like a photograph, too, so that we can see what he or she looks like. Armed with the information you provide (together with your feedback), we can adjust the ingredients and quantities on an ongoing basis so as to best meet your dog's needs.

The ordering process

You can order online or by telephone. After you supply us with your dog's details and preferences, we make up his or her food in our kitchens and freeze it.

The next stage is packing and shipping. The food, bones and treats are placed into separate containers and labelled. This is then packed (together with feeding notes) into insulated, recyclable boxes and despatched to you using an overnight delivery service. Our packaging keeps food cool for up to 48 hours.

When the shipment arrives, we ask you to take it out of the box and put it into your freezer. We suggest that before going to bed every night you simply remove the following day's food from the freezer so that it has a chance to defrost.

We ask you to keep us up to date with any changes in your dog's health or lifestyle so that we can adjust his or her diet if necessary. A week before we are due to make up the next month's supply we contact you to check everything we plan meets with your agreement and then we repeat the whole process.

Excellent value for money

It costs much less than you might expect to feed your dog with Honey's. We keep the cost down by dealing direct with our customers (so no profit to retailers or wholesalers). The price is linked to the exact weight of your dog and will be calculated for you as part of the order process. Our policy is to charge less than you would pay for the identical ingredients if you purchased them from an ethical supplier, such as Waitrose, Riverford or Able & Cole.

Our 100% money-back guarantee

We are proud to say that almost all our customers come to us by word of mouth. In order to ensure that we maintain our reputation for quality, service and integrity we guarantee that your food will arrive in first class condition on the promised date. If you are dissatisfied with the quality of our food simply follow the instructions in the delivery box and we will refund the cost in full and without argument.

Never worry about running out

Assuming you and your dog are happy with Honey's, we will set up a regular order for you so that you never have to worry about running out.

Our Chief Veterinary Surgeon designs and approves all our food

When you feed your dog Honey's you can rest assured that his or her diet has been designed and approved by our own Chief Veterinary Surgeon, Tom Farrington MVB MRCVS VetMFHom.

Tom is an honours veterinarian, holds an advanced degree in Veterinary Homeopathy, has over 28 years of experience in practice, lectures regularly and is responsible for creating an innovative range of homeopathic remedies called Homeopet (www.homeopet.com).

Tom has been encouraging owners to switch their dogs (and cats) to a raw food diet for over two decades. Since then he has seen the practical benefits in thousands of cases.

Tom is responsible for devising all our formulas. He stipulates which ingredients should be used and in what proportions as well as providing guidance as to what volume of food to be fed each day. Thanks to him, you can be confident that Honey's Real Dog Food provides the right nutritional balance for your dog.

Free veterinary consultation, without obligation

If you are worried about your dog's health, a change of diet could really make a huge difference. One of our retained vets, vetinary nurses or nutritionists will be delighted to review your dog's health issues and make dietary recommendations. You will be under no obligation to accept their suggestions and no charge will be made. Where our consultant recommends a raw diet (and this isn't automatic, as they are all completely independent), we will happily quote for preparing it for you.

We are deeply concerned about animal welfare

All the meat we use is free-range and/or organic or (in the case of the game) wild. We are concerned about the welfare of the animals we use to make our food. We know and trust all the farmers we buy from. Our objective is to keep 'dog food miles' to a minimum. We try to source everything from local, ethical farmers. By 'local', we mean as close to our kitchens in Pewsey as possible. When ingredients are hard to source locally we may have to go further afield (up to Wales, for instance). We never, ever source ingredients that are not from mainland Britain. We won't touch factory-farmed animals.

All our dog food is suitable for human consumption

It isn't just that our ingredients must pass the 'suitable for human consumption' test: they must be of the highest quality we can find. We don't buy anything that we wouldn't be happy to cook for our own families.

About the business

Our kitchens are based in the depths of rural Wiltshire and we source our ingredients from small, local suppliers.

Our offices are just up the lane from Vicky's home (she's our managing director), and so you may sometimes hear dogs and children in the background when you call. We aren't a big venture and this allows us to offer a genuinely personal service. In fact, we must be the only dog food company in the world that knows just about every single one of its canine customers by name.

We donate 1% of sales to Compassion in World Farming

We donate 1% of all our sales to Compassion in World Farming (CIWF). This is because we believe that the low standard of farm animal welfare both in the UK and elsewhere is one of the greatest scandals in modern human history. CIWF was founded in 1967 by a British farmer who became horrified by the development of modern, intensive factory farming. Today it strives peacefully to end all cruel factory farming practices. Its campaigning has resulted in the EU recognising animals as sentient beings, capable of feeling pain and suffering. It has also secured landmark agreements to outlaw the barren battery cage for egg-laying hens, narrow veal crates and sow stalls across Europe. We like the fact that CIWF generally works with business, not against it.

Just looking for ethically sourced ingredients?

If you want to prepare your own raw food then we can supply you with a range of ethically sourced raw ingredients along with full instructions.

The choice changes according to the season but generally includes carcasses (chicken, turkey, duck &c.), raw meaty bones, heart (ox, lamb, beef &c.), liver, tripe (washed in water), chicken wings, necks (chicken, turkey &c.) and even sheep heads.

If you are new to raw feeding, we usually recommend that you begin with our made-up food and then, once you have got the hang of it, start to make the switch. All our raw ingredients are suitable for human consumption.

Please, please remember we are happy to offer free advice

Our main objective at Honey's is to encourage people to switch their dogs to a natural diet. We will happily help you with free advice, tips and recipes even if there is never, ever any chance that you will become a customer. Please don't hesitate to contact us if you feel we can help you.

How to get in touch with Honey's

By telephone
01672 620 260

By email
info@honeysrealdogfood.com

By post
Honey's Real Dog Food
Darling's House
1-3 Salisbury Road
Pewsey
Wiltshire SN9 5PZ

Or visit our website
www.honeysrealdogfood.com

Image Credits

Nearly all the black and white photos in this book are the property of Getty Images, and are used here under license. Listings refer to the chapter number facing page.

1. **Imagno**, c.1930. *A dog jumps through hoops at a dog-show in Sussex.* [photograph] (Hulton Archive).
2. **Fox Photos.** *Dog And Cat Car.* [photograph] (Hulton Archive).
3. **Imagno**, 1937. *A dog in the Hyde-Park in London jumps into the cool water.* [photograph] (Hulton Archive).
4. **Willie Vanderson**, 1960. *Nine Puppy Mother.* [photograph] (Hulton Archive).
5. **BIPs**, 1975. *Canine Banquet.* [photograph] (Hulton Archive).
6. **Hulton Collection**, 1935. *Dog's Dinner.* [photograph] (Hulton Archive).
7. **Hulton Collection**, 1935. *Doggy Tricks.* [photograph] (Hulton Archive).
8. **Hulton Collection**, 1925. *Rambling Gold.* [photograph] (Hulton Archive).
9. **Keystone**, 1954. *Dog Carrying Cups.* [photograph] (Hulton Archive).
10. **General Photographic Agency**, 1927. *Performing Dog.* [photograph] (Hulton Archive).
11. **Three Lions**, 1955. *Feeding Time.* [photograph] (Hulton Archive).
12. **Hulton Collection**, 1950. *Puppy wrapped in towel (B&W).* [photograph] (Hulton Archive).
13. **General Photographic Agency**, 1935. *Dog Tired.* [photograph] (Hulton Archive).
14. **Michael Lawn**, 1959. *Doggy Reader.* [photograph] (Hulton Archive).
15. **Shorpy**, 1930. *Timmons.* [photograph] (Creative Commons).
16. **Hulton Collection**, 1978. *Dog and Bone.* [photograph] (Hulton Archive).
17. **Three Lions**, 1955. *Catch it Spotty!* [photograph] (Hulton Archive).

215878MX